"Jani Ortlund has once again written a convicting work for women seeking after God. [illegible] each of the Ten Commandments and challenges us to do som[illegible] fully demonstrates the powerful relevance the commandments hold for Christians who seek holiness by the power of the Holy Spirit."

—Mary K. Mohler, wife of R. Albert Mohler Jr.

"[illegible] Ortlund blows the dust off the stone tablets of the Ten Commandments. Written with the wisdom and insight gained through [illegible] of teaching God's Word and raising four children who love the Lord, *His Loving Law, Our Lasting Legacy* equips readers not only to [illegible] themselves in the revealing light of God's Law, but also to guide children into loving God with their lives."

—Nancy Guthrie, Bible teacher; author, *Holding On to Hope* and *Hoping for Something Better*

"Ortlund explores the richness of God's grace to us and to our children in each of the Ten Commandments. Her warm, devotional style helps move us to respond to God's love by obeying his laws. The creative children's exercises provide engaging questions, crafts, and memorable metaphors that will help children to understand more fully our covenantal God and his Word to us. Any parent or adult who ministers with children will find here a rich curriculum."

—Dr. Tasha Chapman, associate dean of student life; adjunct professor of educational ministries, Covenant Theological Seminary

"Jani Ortland takes us right to the heart of God and offers biblical principles for us to practice and to pass on to our children, so that we may live according to God's law."

—Margi Galloway, minister to women, Scottsdale Bible Church, Arizona

His LOVING LAW *Our* LASTING LEGACY

His Loving Law *Our* Lasting Legacy

Living the Ten Commandments and Giving Them to Our Children

Jani Ortlund

Crossway Books
Wheaton, Illinois

His Loving Law, Our Lasting Legacy: Living the Ten Commandments and Giving Them to Our Children

Published by Crossway Books
a publishing ministry of Good News Publishers
1300 Crescent Street
Wheaton, Illinois 60187

Cover design: Georgia Bateman

Cover photo: iStock

Printed in the United States of America

All emphases in Scripture quotations have been added by the author.

Library of Congress Cataloging-in-Publication Data
Ortlund, Jani
His Loving Law, Our Lasting Legacy : Living the Ten Commandments and Giving Them to Our Children / Jani Ortlund.
p. cm.
ISBN 13: 978-1-58134-868-2 (tpb)
1. Ten commandments. 2. Christian education—Home training. I. Title.
BV4655.O78 2007
241.5'2—dc22 2006102867

CH 17 16 15 14 13 12 11 10 09 08 07
15 14 13 12 11 10 9 8 7 6 5 4 3 2 1

To my beloved mother-in-law

ANNE ORTLUND.

Thank you for a lifetime of loving God
with all your heart
and giving his Word with all your strength.

Your legacy lives on.

CONTENTS

THE TEN COMMANDMENTS

Exodus 20:3–17

1. "You shall have no other gods before me."
2. "You shall not make for yourself a carved image. . . . For I the LORD your God am a jealous God."
3. "You shall not take the name of the LORD your God in vain."
4. "Remember the Sabbath day, to keep it holy."
5. "Honor your father and your mother."
6. "You shall not murder."
7. "You shall not commit adultery."
8. "You shall not steal."
9. "You shall not bear false witness against your neighbor."
10. "You shall not covet . . . anything that is your neighbor's."

Memory Verses

Open my eyes, that I may behold wondrous things out of your law.

Psalm 119:18

"Take to heart all the words by which I am warning you today, that you may command them to your children, that they may be careful to do all the words of this law. For it is no empty word for you, but your very life."

Deuteronomy 32:46–47

You shall love the Lord your God with all your heart and with all your soul and with all your mind. This is the great and first commandment. And a second is like it: You shall love your neighbor as yourself. On these two commandments depend all the Law and the Prophets.

Matthew 22:37–40

INTRODUCTION

AND GOD SPOKE

Praise the L*ORD!*
Blessed is the man who fears the L*ORD,*
who greatly delights in his commandments!
His offspring will be mighty in the land;
the generation of the upright will be blessed.

PSALM 112:1-2

"His offspring will be mighty in the land . . . blessed." What mother doesn't hope that for her children? Raising up children who are leaders both in and outside their homes, respected, courageous, and surrounded by God's blessing is a parent's deepest desire.

The psalmist, inspired by the Holy Spirit, tells us that one of the keys to raising godly, mighty, blessed children is found in a man's fearing the Lord and taking great delight in his commandments. Why should we? How can we? That is the message of this book.

His Loving Law, Our Lasting Legacy will invite you into deeper delight in God as we consider how he loves us through the Ten Commandments. The purpose of this book is to help you pass on that delight to the children in your world.

INTRODUCTION

All These Words

> And God spoke all these words, saying, "I am the LORD your God, who, brought you out of the land of Egypt, out of the house of slavery." (Exodus 20:1–2)

It had been three months since the children of Israel had been rescued from their slavery to Pharaoh. In that short time they had:

- witnessed the miracles of the plagues and the Passover (Exodus 7:1–12:32);
- been led by the steadfast love of the Lord as he went before them in a pillar of cloud by day and a pillar of fire by night (Exodus 13:17–22);
- experienced a never-to-be repeated deliverance from their enemies as the Egyptian army was swallowed up in the Red Sea (Exodus 14:5–30);
- tasted the bitter water turned sweet at Marah (Exodus 15:22–25);
- enjoyed much-needed rest at the oasis of Elim (Exodus 15:27);
- feasted on manna and quail each morning and evening (Exodus 16);
- drunk freely of water springing suddenly from a rock at Meribah (Exodus 17:1–7); and
- watched as Joshua and some of their own men defeated the Amalekites by the power of God (Exodus 17:8–13).

Then God led them to their new camp at Mount Sinai. What would he do after all these miracles? He *spoke* to them. From the midst of thunders and lightnings and a thick cloud and a very loud trumpet blast and a mountain that trembled greatly (Exodus 19), God spoke to his children. When God speaks, it is better than any miracle. What should we do with his words?

The first thing we should do is *listen* to his words. "Everyone who is of the truth listens to my voice" (John 18:37). Thoughtful, patient listening to the message of God's grace in Christ leads us into a fresh knowledge of him. Listening is communing with God. It is seeing reality from his perspective.

God built the human heart with all its desires and needs. His law not only shows us who he is, but it also gives us deep and profound insights into who we are. Donald Grey Barnhouse explained it this way:

> The law of God is like a mirror. Now the purpose of a mirror is to reveal to you that your face is dirty, but the purpose of a mirror is not to wash your face. When you look in a mirror and find that your face is dirty, you do not then reach to take the mirror off the wall and attempt to rub it on your face as a cleansing agent. The purpose of the mirror is to drive you to water.[1]

Jesus is that water (John 4:10, 14). As the law reveals our deceitful and sick hearts (Jeremiah 17:9), we are tempted to withdraw in either pride or defeat. But Jesus invites us to draw near to God as he washes us with water made pure by his perfect fulfillment of the law and his God-satisfying punishment for our failure to keep it (Hebrews 10:19–22). The law drives us to the perfect Law Keeper to have the guilt of our law breaking rinsed away by the living water.

The second thing we should do is *love* his words. "Oh how I love your law! It is my meditation all the day" (Psalm 119:97). "The law of your mouth is better to me than thousands of gold and silver pieces" (v. 72). Open, eager cherishing of God's words leads us into deeper intimacy with him. Loving his words is experiencing life in his presence.

The God of the Bible is a God of the heart who brought his children out of slavery (Exodus 19:4), leading them with cords of kindness and bands of love (Hosea 11:4), and redeeming them in love and pity (Isaiah 63:9). He is the God who sent us Jesus, his beloved Son, who lived a life of delighting in God's commandments and showed us what real love looks like, for at the core of all that God is, is love (1 John 4:16). His love is the supreme energy of the universe. It is this love that draws us into fellowship with him, leading us out of the Egypt of our sins and, in love and pity, redeeming us from our own personal slavery in the kingdom of darkness (Romans 8:34–35).

The third thing we should do is *leave* his words. His words are for listening, for loving, and also for leaving a legacy to the children in our lives. "You shall teach them diligently to your children, and shall talk of them when you sit . . . walk . . . lie . . . and . . . rise . . ." (Deuteronomy 6:7). "We will not hide them from their children, but tell to the coming generation the glorious deeds of the LORD, and his might, and the wonders that he has done" (Psalm 78:4). Intentional, insightful teaching of God's words brings our families into a sacred accountability with God. It is passing on a way of life that will last forever. If the strength and vibrancy and stability of the church depends on the children of our churches in the coming years, what will her future be? The church is always only one generation away from extinction.

Susan Hunt has said that children are a product of their theology.[2] How true! What theology are you living out before the children in your life? What kind of God do your actions, your words, your responses to daily life show them?

As you work through this book, God will be speaking to you. Let his words instruct you, motivate you, and claim you and your family for Christ. At the end of each chapter you will find questions for study and discussion. After you read each chapter, stop and reflect, perhaps with a friend or in a small group, about what you are learning. Let the mirror of God's loving law and the living water flowing from Jesus Christ open the door for deeper delight in our Law Giver.

HIS LOVING LAW

GRACE BEFORE LAW

The prologue to the Ten Commandments (Exodus 20:1–2) teaches us how God deals with his children: "I am the LORD your God, who brought you out of the land of Egypt, out of the house of slavery." The law belongs in a context of grace. We see this in the fact that the law doesn't come until chapter 20 of Exodus. The preceding nineteen chapters tell the story of God's grace as the bedrock of his relationship with us.

When the sons and daughters of Israel asked why they were taught to keep God's law, their parents told them the story of their rescue from slavery by God's mighty hand, as they had been instructed (Deuteronomy 6:20–25). The only way they could understand the meaning of the law was by knowing its context, which was the experience of the exodus, the story of their salvation. First grace, then law.[3] Grace does not undermine law. Grace is the larger wrap-around truth explaining why the law deserves a wholehearted "yes!" from every one of us.

God is not speaking out of a void. He is intimately connected with his people. When he says in Exodus 20:2, "I am the LORD your God, who brought you out of the land of Egypt, out of the house of slavery," he is describing each believer's salvation. Our exodus is his power bringing us out of our captivity to sin and guilt so that we would live for him. He is our freedom fighter.

Christ obeyed the law perfectly in our place. He died a guilty death in our place. And when God, through the sacrifice of his beloved Son, sets his lavish grace upon us, he claims our loyalty. His loving law shows us how to live out that loyalty.

His Treasured Possession

In the prologue to his Ten Commandments, God lays claim to you and me. That's the point! He is the Lord *your* God who brought *you* out of *your* Egypt. If you know Jesus Christ, your conversion was your exodus out of your personal slavery and into covenant with "him who called you out of darkness into his marvelous light" (1 Peter 2:9). God is saying, "I am establishing a love relationship with you by my all-forgiving, all-providing grace. I commit myself to you. Now commit yourself to me, and you will be my treasured possession" (Exodus 19:3–6; 1 Peter 2:9–10). And now he is writing his law on your heart (Jeremiah 31:31–34), and his abundant grace makes his law "sweeter also than honey" (Psalm 19:10) and "not burdensome" (1 John 5:3).

Made to Worship

Every human being was made to worship, and we all worship something:

- money
- control
- food
- success

- pleasure
- beauty
- reputation
- you name it!

Whatever I worship becomes my master. I am the slave of whatever I live for or whatever I cannot live without. Whatever drives me has authority over me. The Bible says, "Whatever overcomes a person, to that he is enslaved" (2 Peter 2:19).

The human heart has room for only one master. You are either serving Christ or another master. When Christ becomes your master, nothing else can master you. "No servant can serve two masters" (Luke 16:13). The law shows us which master we are *really* serving, and it teaches the redeemed of the Lord how to live for their new Master.

God's concern is to keep the one who has been liberated from falling back into slavery. The real meaning of our freedom is obedience to Christ. The Ten Commandments "are rules of life for liberated people."[4] When Jesus frees you from the ugliness and grief of your sins, he relocates you where you can enjoy his liberation—and that is obedience.

We mustn't think of the Ten Commandments as just a list of dos and don'ts. When we do, they become their own form of slavery. The law of God is not slavery. God doesn't lead us out of one kind of slavery only to drive us into another!

But neither does freedom mean erasing all restrictions. We all live quite happily—even freely—in a world filled with boundaries. We can't live under water; we mustn't go barefoot in the snow or play catch with a burning coal. I would recommend using an elevator rather than a window to come to ground level safely, and we are all grateful for traffic signals—at least when we've got the green light! True freedom is enjoying Christ within the boundaries of his kingdom because, "He has delivered us from the domain of darkness and transferred us to the kingdom of his beloved Son" (Colossians 1:13).

Does the law restrict us? Sure it does—the way the sky restricts an eagle, or the soil confines a seed, or the ocean cramps a minnow. Embrace God's law as his loving pathway for you out of sin's slavery and into true freedom—freedom to live life well in the kingdom of his beloved Son.

OUR LASTING LEGACY

Living the Law

Imagine this: you are staying for a week in a rented apartment. In the bathroom there is an extra door on which is posted this sign:

PLEASE DO NOT OPEN THIS DOOR
AT ANY TIME DURING YOUR VISIT
Guest Services

What would your response be? This really happened to me! I'll tell you how I responded. At first I was just so curious! "What could possibly be hidden behind this door?" Then my curiosity turned to scorn: "How ridiculous! They ought to find another place for whatever is hidden behind this door." And then as the week wore on, my scorn turned to pride: "So they think I'll fall for this, huh? Just watch—it's probably some sort of *Candid Camera* trick."

I left that week quite proud that I had never opened that forbidden door. My outward obedience, however, didn't really say much about me. Oh sure, I could control my hand from twisting that doorknob for a week. But I couldn't control my heart's scornful itch to disregard this simple request from my host. We live in a day that despises and fears any restrictions imposed by another—divine or human.

As we go through this study we must come to grips with the nature of the human heart. Our rebellious hearts are inclined to perceive the Ten Commandments as unfairly restrictive or as a list of things to do to keep on God's good side. The law does tell us what to do. But more importantly, *it shows us who we are*. The law deals with both the external and the internal. It is like a mirror, showing us our need for cleansing but unable in itself to clean us.

The law tells us to do good and then proves to us that we can't! Righteousness is never humanly manageable. I cannot use the law to produce my own righteousness and somehow gain more of God's favor. As we keep the law, we won't grow in our acceptability (Romans 3:20). But we will grow in blessing (James 1:25). We will go deeper with God than we've ever gone before.

Above all else, the Ten Commandments show us who God is. He is our Savior and Lord. When he gave us the Ten Commandments, he knew that our inability to keep them would lead us to Christ. It is sinners who admire, trust, and embrace a Savior who sets them right with God through his righteousness (Romans 7:7–10; 2 Corinthians 5:21). As you live out his loving law, don't let any misunderstanding of it crush you rather than rescue you. The law is meant to show you who God is and how deeply he can liberate you.

Two Responses

As we come to God's law, we all are faced with one of two responses. Either we will feel that God is too hard of a master, and we will withdraw into a moral universe of our own making where we write our own laws (Judges 2:12; 21:25), or we will turn to God, who offers us Christ as the perfect Savior of sinners. When we do, our guilt over that image in the mirror of his law will turn to true sorrow and repentance. And God will begin doing a deep work in each heart that has turned to him.

God will show you that every violation of the law you have ever committed—or ever will commit—has been absorbed by Christ on the cross of Calvary. God accepts you because he is satisfied with his Son's sacrifice in your place. Not only that, but God will put his very Spirit within you. And his Spirit will get to work, breaking the reign of sin's power in your life. He will transform you into a law-loving servant of God (Ezekiel 36:26–27; Romans 8:1–4; Hebrews 13:20–21), who makes much of Christ's transforming power and little of your obedience. And he will guide you right on through to heaven, where you will keep God's law perfectly (2 Peter 3:13; Revelation 21:27).

Giving the Law

How can we live and give the Ten Commandments in such a way that our homes, our churches, and our cities feel the blessing of God? We must let our children see and feel our love for Christ and his law. The coming generations need to observe in us a wholehearted response to God and his Word to us—a careful, loving obedience that clings to him with all our heart and soul. "Only be very careful to observe the commandment and the law that Moses the servant of the LORD commanded you, to love the LORD your God, and to walk in all his ways and to keep his commandments and to cling to him and to serve him with all your heart and with all your soul" (Joshua 22:5).

Make it your goal to both *inform* and *inflame* your children with your own delight in following Christ. "Blessed is the man . . . [whose] delight is in the law of the LORD, and on his law he meditates day and night" (Psalm 1:1–2).

The Bible tells of wicked Queen Athaliah who, in her pursuit of power, ordered all her children and grandchildren to be killed (2 Kings 11). Only one-year-old Joash escaped. In six short but formative years, young Joash emerges as one of Judah's brightest reformers. *Someone* was influencing this child toward God in those early years. Second Kings 12:2 tells us, "[Joash] did what was right in the eyes of the LORD all his days, because Jehoiada the priest instructed him." Jehoiada gave himself to the training of a young child, and all Judah benefited.

What child needs your influence, your instruction, your example to help him live for Christ in his generation? What legacy are we leaving for the coming generations? When our houses are sold and our possessions divided between our family and Goodwill, what will we have left to the children in our lives?

He . . . appointed a law in Israel,
which he commanded our fathers
to teach to their children,
that the next generation might know them,
the children yet unborn,
and arise and tell them to their children,
so that they should set their hope in God
and not forget the works of God,
but keep his commandments." (Psalm 78:5–7)

What are you leaving your children? What will they remember you with? What will they remember you for? Use the suggestions after each chapter to help the children in your life "set their hopes in God." The discussion questions for "Giving the Ten Commandments to Our Children" can be readily adapted to different age groups.

My prayer is that as you read and discuss *His Loving Law, Our Lasting Legacy* the Lord will direct your heart to the love of God (2 Thessalonians 3:5) and that your offspring will be mighty in the land (Psalm 112:1–2).

INTRODUCTION

STUDY AND DISCUSSION FOR LIVING THE TEN COMMANDMENTS

1. Read 2 Peter 2:19. What overcomes you? What discourages, distracts, or overwhelms you?

2. Imagine your funeral service. List five attributes you would like others to use to describe your influence in their lives.

   1. ____

   2. ____

   3. ____

   4. ____

   5. ____

If you had only three possessions to pass down to the next generation, what would they be?

   1. ____

   2. ____

   3. ____

3. Review the story of Exodus chapters 1–19, focusing on God's loving care. Now read Exodus 20:1–2, inserting your name in place of the words *your* and *you*.

4. God is speaking to us in the Ten Commandments. What are three things God wants us to do with his words?

   1. ____
   Genesis 3:1; Exodus 15:26; Proverbs 22:17; Matthew 17:5; 1 John 4:6

   2. ____
   Psalm 1:2; 19:10; 119:72, 97

3. ____

Deuteronomy 6:6–7; 32:46–47; Psalm 71:17–18; 78:4

5. How does God love us through his law? See Deuteronomy 7:6–11 and Psalm 19:7–11.

6. Describe how God's law is like a mirror. What can a mirror do? What can't a mirror do?

7. Meditate on Jeremiah 17:9–10. Take time to talk with God about your heart's condition. Pray over Jeremiah 31:33 and Psalm 51:10. Ask God to write his law deep within your own heart.

8. To ponder and pray over: what would a family look like in which the Ten Commandments were making a lasting impact? How about a church, a classroom, a city, or a country?

9. Memorize Psalm 119:18. Use it as your prayer as you study God's loving law. "Open my eyes, that I may behold wondrous things out of your law."

INTRODUCTION

STUDY AND DISCUSSION FOR GIVING THE TEN COMMANDMENTS TO OUR CHILDREN

Materials needed: Bible, pencil, marker, large piece of red poster paper, scissors, index cards, small mirror, and tape.

1. Does your child know the story of Moses and the exodus? Look through a children's Bible together to teach or review the events leading up to the giving of the Ten Commandments. As you set the stage for this study, make sure your child understands the Israelites' slavery to the Egyptians and God's wonderful deliverance that brought them to Mount Sinai. The depth of this review will depend on your child's age and attention span. But the important concept is that God was freeing his people from slavery, and they needed to know how to live in that freedom. Talk much about God's personal love and care for his people (Isaiah 63:9; 1 John 3:1). Discuss, if appropriate, how people today can still be in slavery—a different kind of slavery (to food, money, fame). Then read Exodus 20:1–2, inserting your child's name—and your name—in place of the words *your* and *you*.

2. How does God speak to us today? This is a wonderful opportunity to teach your child about God's Holy Word given to us long ago and preserved through the ages. Also talk about why we have pastors and Bible teachers. Discuss what we should do when God speaks.

   ____

   Matthew 17:5; John 18:37; 1 John 4:3, 6

   ____

   Psalm 119:72, 97

   ____

   Psalm 78:4

   Show your child that you are under God's authority, too, and that you are obeying God when you teach your child God's Word (Deuteronomy 6:6–7). Let her see that it is your delight to obey your heavenly Father. Does your child see spiritual delight in you? Is she growing up sensing that Christ is your treasure above all else? Does your child see you listening carefully and loving wholeheartedly "all these words" that God speaks to you?

3. Draw a huge heart on red poster paper. Have your child cut it out and tape a small mirror in the center. Without your child noticing, put some soot from a burned-out match or a candlewick on your hand and then lovingly touch your child's face so that some rubs off. Have him look in the mirror on the big red heart. Ask your child, "What are mirrors for? Can we use this mirror to clean ourselves?" Discuss how the law is like a mirror, showing us how dirty we are in our thoughts and actions. (Think of how messy we would be if we never had a mirror to check how we looked before we left our homes each morning!) The law reminds us of our need for cleansing and sends us to Jesus, the living water, who cleanses our hearts (John 4:13–14; Hebrews 10:19–22).

4. Read Psalm 14:2–3 and Romans 3:10 together with your child. Talk about sin. What is sin? Make sure your child understands the expressions—"no, not one" and "not even one"—in these verses. Tell him your own personal testimony. How has sin affected your life? How has it affected his? Don't let sin shock you. Our response as parents should never be "How could you?" or "Why did you?" or "What were you thinking?" because every single human being is caught in a nasty web of sin. How could he answer those questions other than "I'm included in the 'not even one' of Psalm 14:3"? Read Jeremiah 17:9–10 and copy it on an index card. Attach it to the very top of your heart above the mirror.

5. Do not leave your child here. A child's heart is very open to her own evil and her need for a savior (Matthew 18:2–4). Tell your child about Jesus' love for her (Mark 10:13–16). Read Jeremiah 31:33. Pray over this truth with your child. Write, "I will put my law within them, and I will write it on their hearts," on another index card and tape it right under the small mirror.

6. Memorize Psalm 119:18 together. Make this your prayer as you study the Ten Commandments. Find a prominent place where you can hang your big red heart as you do this study with your child.

CHAPTER ONE

NO OTHER GODS

"You shall have no other gods before me."

EXODUS 20:3

Ray and I travel a lovely twelve-mile drive along a country road to get to our church. But I often arrive feeling rather guilty. Why do I treat the 40 mph speed sign as just a suggestion from my local sheriff? Depending on how late I leave home on a Sunday morning, 45 to 50 mph will do quite nicely for me, thank you.

We live in a day where our sense of self is elevated to such a degree that our sense of personal responsibility has almost vanished. We always have good, justifiable reasons for what we do. "Someone else may be guilty, but not me!"

William Kilpatrick relates a story from a Boston College colleague: "[My colleague] told me that he once asked members of his philosophy class to write an anonymous essay about a personal struggle over right and wrong, good and evil. Most of the students, however, were unable to complete the assignment. 'Why?' he asked [them]. 'Well,' they said—and apparently this was said without irony—'We haven't done anything wrong.' We can see a lot of self-esteem here, but very little self-awareness."[1]

The Ten Commandments bring us face-to-face with our inner

reality. We have seen that the law is like a mirror, reflecting to us our imperfections and failures. And it is a good mirror, clear and true. We need it. "Who can discern his errors?" (Psalm 19:12). "The heart is deceitful above all things, and desperately sick; who can understand it?"(Jeremiah 17:9). Do we believe God's description of our hearts? Do you believe this is true of your heart, and your child's heart? Our hearts are worse than we know.

A mirror is only useful to someone who looks into it with eyes opened. There is real evil in this world. But there is a deeper truth to be told. The Bible says there is real evil in our souls (Romans 3:9–19), and the law of God reveals it.

The law's purpose, however, is deeper than providing a mirror for moral reflection. The law is meant to draw us to the One who can cleanse what we see in that mirror, and in that cleansing, win our hearts, so that we learn to love and obey his law. "I will run in the way of your commandments when you enlarge my heart!" (Psalm 119:32). "Lead me in the path of your commandments, for I delight in it" (Psalm 119:35).

Grace precedes law. The first nineteen chapters of Exodus are full of God's gracious care for the children of Israel. "I am the Lord your God, who . . ." The entire story up to this point has been grace. For eighteen chapters, all the way to Mount Sinai, it is God who acted, God who cared, and God who rescued these slaves and made them into a people. God took the initiative over and over again. That is what his grace does for us—it rescues us from what we can't do on our own. God's grace is a massive rescue operation.

And grace should never be a passive force in the life of a believer. We are shaped by grace from start to finish. It should activate and liberate us. The nature of God's grace energizes and inspires his children.

Do you remember those days as a child when you so wanted to buy your father a Father's Day gift but had no money of your own? If you were like me, you would go to your dad and ask for some cash. He would ask you what you needed it for, and when you told him, he would smile, reach into his pocket, and give you the money.

Sometimes he would even drive you to the store to spend it. And on Father's Day, around the dinner table, in all sincerity he would make much of your present. Your gift was from him and for him and to him—grace from start to finish.

HIS LOVING LAW

In Exodus 20:1–2 God reminds Israel of his redeeming grace. They belong to him now. He has loved them and redefined his relationship to them, essentially saying, "Do you remember who you were? You were slaves, but now you are my people. I value you."

The first commandment called for an undivided love from slaves for their Redeemer. God was calling them out of their familiar world into an exclusive, intimate relationship with him. In the ancient world polytheism was assumed. All the other nations in Israel's day had a smorgasbord of gods and goddesses that they could mix and match and with whom they exchanged loyalties in order to ensure whatever they needed at that time.

The plagues targeted Egypt's various gods (their gods of water and sun, and darkness, and so on, Exodus 12:12) and called for Israel to leave them behind (Ezekiel 20:7–8). God was saying to those he rescued, "I have discredited those gods. I alone am God, and I am your God. You shall have no other gods before me."

THE EXCLUSIVE LOVE OF GOD

What do we see about God in this first commandment? We see that God loves us with an *exclusive* love. The love of God is an intense, specific, passionate love, and, as we'll see when we look at the second commandment, God describes the sort of love he has for us as *jealous* love. He will not share his redeemed son or daughter with another. "You shall worship no other god, for the LORD, whose name is Jealous, is a jealous God" (Exodus 34:14).

God's jealousy over his loved one is not ugly or selfish. His relationship with his redeemed one is exclusive because *intimacy thrives in exclusivity*. The Bible often refers to our relationship with God using a marital metaphor. What husband would tolerate sharing his wife's heart with another? What wife wouldn't want her husband to rise up and call her back to him if another man started demanding her attention?[2] God is saying, "I am giving myself to you in grace. I don't want anything between us. I want to be the sole object of your devotion and allegiance and worship." Do you hear God's loving words to you, his loving jealousy over your heart?

Have you ever walked through the airport listening with half an ear to the messages being repeated over the speaker system? "In the interest of public safety, smoking is confined to the designated areas . . . There is no parking along the curb . . . All parked cars will be towed at the owner's expense . . . Paging Mrs. Jani Ortlund. . . ." (Wait a minute—they just called *my* name!) "Mrs. Ortlund, please proceed to the nearest white courtesy phone for an important message." We ignore the messages until they speak our name!

In this commandment, God is speaking your name. He is saying, "____, I have called you and brought you to myself. I have redeemed you from your own personal Egypt. And I am jealous for your heart. I want you to love me above everything else. I want your undivided love. You shall have no other gods before me."

God is single, whole. He gives himself wholly. He hates division, whether between brothers (Proverbs 6:19), or in his tabernacle (Exodus 26:6), and most especially in our hearts (1 Chronicles 28:9; Psalm 73:25). His grace demands our undivided love. Through this first command God is protecting and nurturing his intense, exclusive love relationship with his beloved.

The Loving Exposure of Other Gods

You may be thinking, "I don't have any other gods. For goodness's sake, I am a Christian. Is this even relevant today?" But remember to whom this command was written—to God's redeemed. God was speaking to his own children. The very wording of it acknowledges that there are other gods whom we do and will worship. God wouldn't warn us against things that don't exist.

The truth is we do have other gods. We don't actually eliminate God, but we allow god substitutes to cohabit beside him. These may not be full-sized replacements for God, but we become increasingly attached to them, making God remote.[3]

Anything that comes between God and us that compromises our walk with him *is a god to us*. We are saying, "You're not really enough for this situation, Lord. You are not providing for me or protecting me or fulfilling me in the ways that I need, so I am bringing this other god into my life to close the gap between your inadequacy and my needs."

You don't need to be kneeling before a tangible idol to be enslaved. "Whatever overcomes a person, to that he is enslaved" (2 Peter 2:19). How do you know if something is overwhelming, or enslaving, you? Well, consider this:

- Where do you turn in times of trouble?
- When you are lonely or discouraged, what is your first source of comfort?
- What do you love and admire and honor?
- What excites you?
- What do you spend your money on and invest your time in?
- What is at the very core of your life?

Whatever, whoever, has a hold on your heart—a greater, stronger, seemingly more satisfying hold than Jesus Christ—has become your god. Matthew Henry, a Puritan minister, described our human gods like this:

> Pride makes a god of self, covetousness makes a god of money, sensuality makes a god of the belly; whatever is esteemed or loved, feared, or served, delighted in or depended on more than God, that (whatever it is) we do in effect make a god of.[4]

The Bible gives us examples of these kinds of gods:

- Power: Habakkuk 1:11
- Money: 1 Timothy 6:9–10; Matthew 6:24
- Covetousness (things): Colossians 3:5
- Appetite: Philippians 3:19
- Pleasure: 1 Corinthians 10:7

The ultimate god behind every other god of our heart is self. "For people will be lovers of self . . . rather than lovers of God, having the appearance of godliness, but denying its power" (2 Timothy 3:2–5). Oscar Wilde wrote, "To love oneself is the beginning of a lifelong romance."[5]

How can false worship develop in our heart? It starts with a *cooling* toward God, an indifference, a neglect, that allows our love for God to become lukewarm (Revelation 2:4; 3:16).

This leads to *impatience* with the ways of God, a *dissatisfaction* with his "Godness." We begin charging God foolishly for those things that disappoint us. "How could he let this happen? Why doesn't he answer? If I were God, I would . . ." (Job 40:2, 8). This finally leads to *estrangement* from our heavenly Father because of the idols we have stored in our hearts (Ezekiel 14:1–5).

God is calling to you in this first commandment. He is calling you away from false worship back to himself. The God who brought you out of the Egypt of your old life now claims you. He gave himself fully at the cross. Does any other god deserve your heart?

OUR LASTING LEGACY

Living the First Commandment

Our wholehearted God expects a wholehearted response from us. He tells us that lukewarm Christians make him nauseous (Revelation 3:16). He is saying, "Don't run after foolish, empty gods. Deliberately reject these gods of your own making. I value you. Now learn to value me. Do not receive my grace in vain" (see 2 Corinthians 6:1).

God must be first in the heart of his child. He must be at the very center of our lives. Our desires, motives, actions, finances, sorrows, failures, successes—everything—must come under the declaration, "You are my God. I will not share my heart with any other."

How do we live this out? We begin, with God's help, to *undeify* the other gods in our lives. We no longer base our happiness and fulfillment on Jesus *plus* anything—a husband, children, reputation, house, health, achievements. *What if God were the only thing you had in heaven and earth?* Is he enough? Could you be happy?

When we choose God as our only God, everything starts to change. We begin to see everything as from God and everything as for God. "I have no good apart from you" (Psalm 16:2). Every task becomes a divine appointment; every meal becomes a feast on his goodness; every dollar earned and spent is gratefully received from the hand of God and yielded to him for his investment; every gift from him is an undeserved grace. We begin to experience authentic Christianity as miracle, not management.

Is your life a miracle? Are you living proof of what God can do, or do you seek to make yourself what you are, even as a Christian?[6] God is saying positively to us in this first commandment, "You shall have *me*." It is only as we value and enjoy Christ more and more that the other gods in our heart begin to lose their grip on us, and the flavor of our faith presses on from management to miracle.

Giving the First Commandment

Let's think about how we can communicate the exclusivity of God to the children in our spheres of influence. This matters urgently today because the world scorns any teaching of the first commandment as intolerant and even dangerous. Our children need to see and hear the biblical alternative to cultural pluralism in our lives and from our mouths.

When God alone is our God, our foremost delight is to say yes to him. The *first* way a parent can give the first commandment is to be a *Christ first* person—in time, in money, in emotions, in moral standards, in church involvement—living out her delight in God's being her only God.

Do our schedules show us living out the first commandment? Do we enjoy Christ enough to spend time with him? Do we say no to other things so that we can linger in his presence? Do we value him enough to give him the best of our time and energy? Is he really our first and highest prize in life and in death (Psalm 63:1–8)?

Do our children see this in us? The primary way you can give this commandment to the next generation is to live out your "yes" to God, saying with your words, your actions, your all, "You, and you alone, are my God." The Westminster Larger Catechism puts it this way in question 104: "What are the duties required in the first commandment?" And the answer given is:

> The duties required in the first commandment are, the knowing and acknowledging of God to be the only true God and our God; and to worship and glorify him accordingly by thinking, meditating, remembering, highly esteeming, honouring, adoring, choosing, loving, desiring, fearing of him; believing in him; trusting, hoping, delighting, rejoicing in him; being zealous for him; calling upon him, giving all praise and thanks and yielding all obedience and submission to him with the whole man; being careful in all things to please him, and sorrowful when in any thing he is offended; and walking humbly with him.[7]

Not only do you need to give the first commandment by example; you also need to give it by teaching your child about the exclusive nature of God's love for him and leading him into a personal encounter with God's Son, Jesus Christ. People (both little people and big people) always relate better to a person, not a mere thing like a law. Salvation is not a thing, an idea, a method. It is a person—Jesus Christ!

Nearly any adult, by virtue of size and strength alone, can get a child to obey outwardly. But our goal should be a changed heart. We want to see our kids motivated by an inner, personal inspiration. Our aim should always be to help them approach God and begin to listen to God himself. Bring your child to the living God over and over again.

Help him form a personal attachment to Jesus Christ. This is the most beautiful and beneficial of all legacies you could ever give a child.

We want to learn how to give the Ten Commandments to our children. A law always commands and prohibits. It governs our actions. A person, on the other hand, speaks, inspires, leads, understands. The message of the Bible is that God is alive. He is a person calling us into a living, personal relationship with him. Do your kids see a parent whose heart is captivated by her God? Are they motivated by your words, your actions, and your responses to life to find their delight in God, too?

The first commandment assumes that we will worship something—either the true God, or our own replacement—because we were made to worship. We love to be wowed, thrilled, dazzled. So do children. All children are born worshipers. From Barney to Britney Spears, a child's heart is captivated by what dazzles him, even at an early age.

As you bring your children to God, let there be no doubt in their minds who thrills you, who is worthy of your awe and worship! Hold out the glories of God to your children. Let them see how much he means to you. Tell your children how deeply you long for them to experience the wonders and delights of God. Don't feed their idols. Feed them from God's Word. Show them the cross, where idolaters are forgiven and liberated. Teach them God's ways and wisdom and rewards.

As you think through this first commandment, remember and remind your children that someday, when you both get to heaven, there will no longer be a struggle in your heart between God and other gods. You will be conformed to the image of his Son. Your whole being will be set apart to God. And you will be caught up in his glory and mercy and grace forever and ever and ever.

"You shall have no other gods before me." This loving law reveals the jealous love of God. It exposes our god substitutes. It calls us to say yes to him and to help our children say yes to God, too. And it holds out the promise of eternal wholehearted communion with the God who is more than enough to satisfy our every desire.

THE FIRST COMMANDMENT

STUDY AND DISCUSSION FOR LIVING THE FIRST COMMANDMENT

1. Review your memory verse, Psalm 119:18. Pray it into your study this week. Memorize Exodus 20:3.

2. Why do you think this is the *first* commandment?

3. What does the exclusive nature of God's love teach us?

4. The students at Boston College could not recognize any personal struggles with right and wrong, good and evil. How, in your pilgrimage thus far, has the grace of God empowered you to reject false gods and give your all to the true God?

5. Think back over the past several months. Looking at your calendar and checkbook, describe what your investment of time and money reveals about the first love in your heart.

6. Read Psalm 19:12 and Jeremiah 17:9. What do you fear, serve, and depend on more than God?

7. Look up these verses and list some things revealed as god substitutes:

   - Habakkuk 1:11
   - 1 Timothy 6:9–10
   - Matthew 6:24
   - Colossians 3:5
   - Philippians 3:19
   - 2 Timothy 3:2–5

Are there other people, desires, things that compete for your spiritual time and energy? Talk to your heavenly Father about this commandment. Meditate on Psalm 62:1 and Matthew 22:36–38. Ask him to fill your heart so full of himself that there is no room for god substitutes.

8. The positive aspect of this first commandment is that we shall have God first and foremost. List everything wonderful you know about God that makes him deserving of such worship.

STUDY AND DISCUSSION FOR GIVING THE FIRST COMMANDMENT TO OUR CHILDREN

Materials needed: Bible, crayons/markers, paper, tape, and the big red heart.

1. Read and memorize the first commandment with your child. Write it on your big red heart.

2. Talk with your child about the meaning of "other gods." Make sure your child understands this is not referring only to carved idols. Read Exodus 34:14 and talk about the exclusive nature of our relationship with God. Talk about all God has done for him:

   - chosen him before the world was even made (Ephesians 1:4–5);
   - formed him in his mother's womb (Psalm 139:11);
   - written every day of your child's life in God's book before your child's life began (Psalm 139:16);
   - prepared good works for your child to do (Ephesians 2:10);
   - sent his Son from heaven to live the perfect life that your child never could, and to die the death that your child deserves, so that he can know God intimately (John 3:16).

3. Talk together about idols. Discuss the nature of idols. Are they only physical? Read 1 Corinthians 6:19–20 and talk about how we let idols into our hearts. Use an illustration from your own life. What idols do children sometimes cultivate?

4. Talk about god substitutes and read Psalm 16:2. Give an example to your child from your own heart. Discuss how even children have god substitutes. If your child can think of one, have him draw a small picture of his god substitute. Draw one of your own, too. Tape them next to the first commandment on your big red heart.

5. Talk about King Solomon from 1 Kings 11:1–10. Solomon started well, but his heart drifted away. What god substitutes did Solomon love more than God?

   1 Kings 6:38 and 1 Kings 7:1______________________________

   Deuteronomy 17:16 and 1 Kings 10:26–29____________________

   1 Kings 11:1–3____

Did these bring Solomon happiness? Read Ecclesiastes 2:4–8, 11, 17.

6. Look for ways to show and tell your child the glories of God (see Psalm 78:4). How does God dazzle you? Why do you admire him? When you are walking, driving, eating, playing, vacationing, and working together, draw attention to the marvels of our great God. Spend time together thinking and praying over the wonders of God. Read Psalms 16:11; 19:1; and 139:7–12 together. At the top of a big piece of paper write Psalm 145:3.

   Spend some time over the next week listing ways God thrills you and your child. Perhaps take some time to illustrate this list. Together write a prayer of praise to our great God.

7. Pray that God would fill your child's heart with a radiance and power that diminishes his god substitutes so that he would set his hope on God (Psalm 78:7).

CHAPTER TWO

ACCEPTABLE WORSHIP

"You shall not make for yourself a carved image . . .
for I the LORD *your God am a jealous God."*

EXODUS 20:4–5

The first and second commandments go together. The first commandment tells us *whom* we should worship. The second commandment tells us *how* we should worship. The first commandment teaches that we must have no *false gods*. The second commandment tells us that we must have no *false worship* of the true God. The first commandment tells us that there can be *no substitute* for God. The second teaches that there must be *no misrepresentations* of the true God. The first commandment shows us the *exclusivity* of our relationship with God. The second commandment tells us of the *magnitude* of that relationship.

The second commandment answers the question, "If Jesus is my only God, how can I worship him, serve him, and represent him according to his Word alone?"

HIS LOVING LAW

God's Zeal for His Beloved

How we worship matters to God. Do you know that there is an acceptable way to worship God? "Let us offer to God acceptable worship, with reverence and awe, for our God is a consuming fire" (Hebrews 12:28–29). "For the LORD your God is a consuming fire, a jealous God" (Deuteronomy 4:24).

The second commandment speaks of the only acceptable way to worship the true and living God. Isn't he kind to communicate what true worship looks like? This is God's loving law to us. In this commandment God is defining his love relationship with his children. God is jealous for my worship because he is in love with me. He is jealous in the way a husband or a caring parent is properly jealous. God's jealousy has to do with his intense, ardent zeal over *my response to his love*. We see this same root word in the Song of Solomon expressed as fervent *love*: "love is strong as death, jealousy is fierce as the grave" (8:6); in Isaiah as the *zeal* of a mighty warrior, stirred up against his foes: "The LORD goes out like a mighty man, like a man of war he stirs up his zeal" (42:13); and elsewhere in Isaiah as his joyful, ever expanding plan of redemption accomplished with his *zeal*: "The zeal of the LORD of hosts will do this" (9:7).

God is never indifferent toward his children. What kind of God would he be if he didn't care about your relationship to him? His jealousy, his zeal for you, is beautiful. In fact, Isaiah prayed for an outpouring of this zeal from God (Isaiah 63:7–9, 15; 64:1). And the prophet Zechariah spoke of the gracious comfort of God's jealousy (Zechariah 1:12–14).

God loves his child with an active, passionate zeal that is meant to be a comfort to us. Such zeal calls for a response in us, and that response is our worship—but we are full of false worship.

Exposing Our False Worship

Think of the Israelites building their golden calf while Moses "delayed" on the mountain with God (Exodus 32:1). They were still fresh from God's gracious and miraculous provision for them. They now lived in full view of God's glory on top of the mountain (Exodus 24:17), yet they wanted something else, something more, something tangible. They were not outright rejecting the Lord. They just wanted God among them in a particular form—a form of their choosing. And so they built the golden calf.

Now jump ahead to the Israelites in the times of the kings. God had filled the temple with his very presence, a glory so powerful that the priests could no longer stand to minister (1 Kings 8:10–11). But into that very temple they set up altars for false gods, "for all the host of heaven" (2 Kings 21:1–9), and God judged them for it (2 Kings 24:1–3).

We think, "How could they?" But we do the same thing. The Bible teaches that our hearts are the temple of God (1 Corinthians 3:16–17; 6:19–20). He wants to reign there alone. But if Jesus Christ is not the all-satisfying treasure of our hearts, we are bringing idols into this temple. Let's think for a minute about what an idol is:

- An idol is any heart-level substitute for God (Ezekiel 14:3).
- An idol is not what I believe, but what I value (Luke 12:34).
- An idol is whatever I use to fill in the blanks in my life where Jesus seems inadequate or unsatisfying (Psalm 62:1).

If you want to do an idol inventory, survey your daydreams and your nightmares. A friend once shared with me these wise words, "An idol is what keeps you up at night." How have you been sleeping lately?

Sin is more profound and goes much deeper than just breaking rules. Sin is worshiping something other than God. Whatever our heart clings to has in fact become our god. False worship is our root problem. And we become like what we worship (2 Kings 17:15). My heart all too easily replaces the living God with cheap substitutes when I tell myself that my joy requires something more than Jesus Christ alone, when I believe Jesus + ____ = my happiness and peace. My expectations of him are so low. So are yours.

There are a lot of things we worship besides God. An idol is a good thing we blow up to be our god. It could be our marriage, or career, or children, or ministry, or home, or health, or endowment, or even a book we are writing!

One of my idols is food. It is my drug of choice. I use food to receive love from others (when I cook a nice meal), or to show love (my pantry is always full when the kids head home for a visit), or to quell anxiety (you should see the bag of M&Ms beside my computer right now as I type!), or to comfort myself, or even to reward myself (I'm thinking about that bowl of chocolate mint ice cream waiting for me when I get this chapter finished).

Of course, nourishment is a legitimate need, and my hunger is a wholesome trigger to meet that need. But when I insist on using food to comfort, soothe, or delight myself—when I think about it constantly, plan for it to an extreme, overspend to satisfy this desire—then food has risen to an ungodly place in my heart. My hunger becomes an idol whenever I use it in an improper way to meet a legitimate need.

Idolatry is not just a problem of long ago. Nor is it only a pagan problem. It is a human problem. Idolatry betrays its presence whenever I respond to human loss or deprivation or hardship with bitterness and anger and sulking. My response proves that I have grounded my happiness in something other than God alone. The second commandment is God's loving law to us because it exposes our false worship.

Teaching Us True Worship

When God commands us not to make for ourselves a carved image, he is not just talking about totem poles and Buddhas. God is teaching us something about himself. He is saying to us, "I am who I am. Let me be all that I am to you."

Images try to represent the deity. But God is saying, "Let me represent myself." We must never try to reduce God to human terms. Learn to see God through his eyes. "To whom then will you liken God, or what likeness compare with him? . . . It is he who sits above the circle of the earth, and its inhabitants are like grasshoppers. . . . To whom then will you compare me, that I should be like him?" (Isaiah 40:18, 22, 25).

We live in a day of the visual. And we long to make the invisible God somehow visible. Think of all the art depicting God through the centuries. Is this wrong? It can be wrong when we make images of God to help us worship him, because that is not how God has chosen to reveal himself, and, therefore, our images can really be only a god of our own making. God tells us not to look, but to listen: "Therefore watch yourselves very carefully. Since you saw no form on the day that the LORD spoke to you at Horeb out of the midst of the fire, beware lest you act corruptly by making a carved image for yourselves, in the form of any figure . . ." (Deuteronomy 4:15–16). Any image we form with our hands or our hearts is inadequate, incomplete, and unworthy of him. There are dangers inherent in any image we make of God.

Let me illustrate it this way. Suppose we became friends through written correspondence. Perhaps you told me a lot about yourself, even describing some of your physical features. Then I decided I would have a gift made for you—a portrait painted of you based solely on our correspondence. Would you be pleased? Would it ever be possible for me to truly represent your likeness on paper, or in any form, without seeing you?

How then could we ever try to represent God in an image of any kind? Images trivialize him, confining him and reducing him to something of our own design. What picture could ever contain a likeness of the Creator of all things? How can we limit God to a picture? God says, "For as the heavens are higher than the earth, so are my ways higher than your ways and my thoughts than your thoughts" (Isaiah 55:9). God is saying, in other words, "Don't try to contain me—I am uncontainable."

Images debase him and degrade him, demeaning him. How could any image reflect God's incomparable power and majesty and glory and beauty and goodness and radiance (Exodus 33:18–19; Revelation 22:5)? Images depersonalize him. How could an image show God's intimacy? He is not tangible to us, but no god is as close as the Lord our God (Psalm 145:18; Matthew 28:20; Hebrews 13:5).

God can never be localized or contained. As my husband says, "God has no edges." No image can possibly be adequate, complete, or worthy. Each type of image can only detail its own misunderstandings. A picture or image tries to communicate God to the worshiper, but God cannot be relegated to an art form.

Who is God that we could represent him in any form (Isaiah 40:21–26)? Think of the vastness of the stars, the brilliance of the sun, the beauty of a rose in bloom, the power of a lightning bolt, the purity of a rainbow. How could we possibly represent God? Job speaks of creation as we know it as the edges of his ways, a faint whisper of God (Job 26:7–14). He is limitless, infinite, immaterial, full of power and majesty, pure and holy—it will take all of eternity to explore who he is.

Jesus tells us that God is spirit and must be worshiped in spirit and in truth (John 4:24). Indeed, "the Father is seeking such people to worship him" (v. 23). God is spiritual in nature. He dwells in unapproachable light and no one has ever seen him or can see him (1 Timothy 6:16).

The second commandment teaches us that we must have no images of God—either physical or mental. It "forbids us to make images of God in our fancies, as if he were a man as we are. Our religious worship must be governed by the power of faith, not by the power of imagination."[1]

Do you try to picture God as you pray or worship? Have you ever said, "I like to think of God as a ____"? J. I. Packer writes:

> How often do we hear this sort of thing: "I *like to think* of God as the great Architect, or Mathematician, or Artist. I don't think of God as a Judge; I *like to think* of Him simply as a Father." We know from experience how often remarks of this kind serve as the prelude to a denial of something that the Bible tells us about God. It needs to be said with the greatest possible emphasis that those who hold themselves free to think of God as they like are breaking the second commandment [emphasis in original].[2]

God does not want us to worship a "godlet" of our own making. A man-made representation of God allows our imaginations too much creative freedom, and we will end up creating God in our own image. That would be exchanging the truth for a lie and worshiping the creature rather than the Creator (Romans 1:25). A picture is always too small, too disappointing.

God does, however, reveal himself to us clearly, though not exhaustively (Exodus 33:19–20). He represents himself as an inextinguishable fire (Exodus 3:2), with a voice like thunder (Exodus 19:19), as a cloud of glory (1 Kings 8:10–11), as a rock, fortress, and shield (Psalm 18:2), as a strong lion (Isaiah 31:4), as an eagle fluttering over its young (Deuteronomy 32:11), and as a shepherd gently tending his flock (Isaiah 40:11), to name just a few.

He has shown us himself in his precious Son. Jesus is "the image of the invisible God" (Colossians 1:15), the "radiance of the glory of God and the exact imprint of his nature" (Hebrews 1:3). He is the only image of God in all of time and space.

And God intends his image to appear in us (Genesis 1:27). The fall diminished God's image in all of Adam's descendants. But God promises us that we will someday bear the image of his Son (Colossians 3:10; Romans 8:29). Jesus is the firstborn among many brothers, and brothers bear a family resemblance.

We are not allowed to make God's image—we are to be his image bearers. You see, God does not hate images, per se. What he hates is a misrepresentation of his glory.

Christianity Is Generational

Another way God loves us through the second commandment is by showing us that there are generational consequences to obeying or disobeying this law. While the Bible teaches that personal responsibility is required in each generation (Ezekiel 18:4, 20), it is also true that we can inherit misery from our fathers. This command is a warning to keep us from sin because our breaches of God's law do affect the next generation. "Human life is interwoven in a web of interaction and mutual influence, for good or for ill. None of us lives solely to ourselves. Our actions impact those nearest and dearest to us."[3]

Think of the impact of adultery or exploitation or drunkenness on the next generation, and then think of the impact of godliness, discipline, purity, and integrity. This is the only commandment where punishment is promised to the coming generations if the command is disobeyed (" . . . visiting the iniquity of the fathers on the children to the third and the fourth generation of those who hate me" [Exodus 20:5]). Why? Because how we worship God determines everything about our relationship with him.

When we refuse to worship God in his way, when we try to recreate an image that is more palatable to us, God says that we *hate* him! The way we worship shows whom we love. But God's passion to bless is greater than his passion to punish (". . . but showing love to a thousand [generations] of those who love me . . ." [Exodus 20:6 NIV]). This commandment is an invitation into his covenant love. It indicates the limitless extent of God's mercy to those who love him. "To thousands of generations" means "to the end of all generations." God's bias is towards love.

OUR LASTING LEGACY

Living the Second Commandment

We have seen that an idol is anything that takes God's place in our hearts. And each of us has idols rooted deeply in our hearts. Our idols are precious to us—but they are also contemptible. Think of the ring in J. R. R. Tolkien's *Lord of the Rings*. Everyone lusted after its power, but whoever wore it suffered under its dehumanizing effect. Middle Earth could only be saved with the destruction of the ring. Tolkien was really saying something. He understood that the key to life is not only what you gain but also what you lose, what you give up, what you throw away.[4]

Paul said, "I have suffered the loss of all things and count them as rubbish, in order that I may gain Christ" (Philippians 3:8). What precious idol have you cherished as essential to your happiness? Has something or someone taken your heart's trust, delight, loyalty, and love besides Jesus Christ? What must you lose in order to gain the only treasure you really cannot live without—Christ?

We are all either idolaters or followers. Either we want to create a god in our image to worship, or we long for God to create his image in us. The Bible says, "Where your treasure is, there your heart will be also" (Matthew 6:21). Our hearts dwell on what we treasure most. What is your first thought in the morning? Your last thought as you are drifting off to sleep? What do you daydream about? Some of us sincerely want God, but we want him on our own terms. We are grateful for him, but there are just some things we can't live without.

God has an alternative to all our idols. His name is Jesus (Isaiah 41:21–42:1). God draws our admiring attention to Jesus, who presents himself to us as our refreshment (Isaiah 41:17). He calls us to dump our idols and to see that we can safely risk all our happiness on him. He is a big God! (Isaiah 41:7–10). He is saying, "Let me prove to you what I can do." The greatest miracle in the universe is that God transforms a compulsive idolater into a passionate worshiper of himself alone.

Come to Jesus. Learn to love the Giver more than the gifts. Learn to make the Lord the center of your universe, the sole satisfaction of your desires.

Each commandment has both a negative and a positive side. God is saying, "Don't bring anything else into your worship of me." And by that he is also saying, "When you truly worship me, you will find me to be enough!"

You were made for God, and only God will do. Don't just try to overpower your idols. Come to God. The more you worship the true God, the more your own images will fade. Seek him with all your heart—that will loosen your grip on your idols. "We know that the Son of God has come and has given us understanding, so that we may know him who is true; and we are in him who is true, in his

Son Jesus Christ. He is the true God and eternal life. Little children, keep yourselves from idols" (1 John 5:20–21).

Giving the Second Commandment

We must teach the coming generations about worship. There are many worship wars going on, splitting families and churches and even denominations. When we talk about a new church, we often do so in terms of whether we liked the worship—is it contemporary or traditional enough for our preferences? Some like old hymns; others prefer new praise choruses. But no one has the corner market on true worship except the One whom we worship. And he has told us that the only worship acceptable to him is that which is spiritual and true (John 4:23–24; Hebrews 12:28–29). That is to be our criteria for where we should worship and what kind of songs we sing—is there truth there?

The law of God is like a mirror. It is also like a lamp (Psalm 119:105). His commandments show us the way forward. The law shows us what we are now, but it also shows us what we will someday be. As you give this commandment to the children in your life, let the light of the gospel lead you to the cross. There you will find truth and life and a way to God so that you may worship him acceptably with all your heart, beginning now and stretching forward into all eternity (Revelation 22:3–5), where there will be no more earthly images, for we will see him face-to-face.

STUDY AND DISCUSSION FOR LIVING THE SECOND COMMANDMENT

1. Review Psalm 119:18. Make this your prayer as you open your Bible to study. Review the first commandment and memorize the second commandment.

2. The Bible speaks repeatedly of God's zeal, his passion, and his ardent interest in his people. Read these verses and describe how God's jealousy over his children is represented in Scripture:

   Song of Solomon 8:6 ______________________________

   Isaiah 42:13 ______________________________

   Isaiah 9:6–7 ______________________________

   Isaiah 63:7–9 ______________________________

   Zechariah 1:12–14 ______________________________

3. What is an idol? Describe some present-day idols.

   Read 1 Corinthians 3:16–17; 6:19–20. What idols are you bringing into God's temple?

4. Why would God forbid us to make any image of him? (Isaiah 40:21–41:1 and Job 26:7–14 will help you to answer.)

5. What are some of the images God gives us of himself in the Bible? Here are a few verses to get you started: Genesis 1:27; Exodus 3:2; 19:17–20; Deuteronomy 32:11; 1 Kings 8:10–11; Psalms 18:2; 23:1;

32:7; Isaiah 31:4–5; 40:11; Matthew 6:9; Ephesians 5:25, 32; Hebrews 1:3; Revelation 5:5; 7:10; 20:11–12.

6. Are you limiting your view of God by confining your thoughts to what you *like* to think about God? In what ways are you a mental idolater?

7. Read Hebrews 12:28–29. Ask God to show you where your worship has been false. Take some time to confess any idols of your heart, along with any images—material or mental—however dear they may be to you.

8. Meditate on Psalm 63:1–8. Open your soul up to God to find real joy and satisfaction.

STUDY AND DISCUSSION FOR GIVING THE SECOND COMMANDMENT TO OUR CHILDREN

Materials needed: Bible, markers, paper and crayons, photograph of a friend or family member your child has not yet met, 3 balloons, pin, tape, and the big red heart.

1. Review with your child how the law is like a mirror, showing us ways that we sin.

2. Review the first commandment (*whom* we worship) with your child, and memorize the second commandment (*how* we worship).

3. Read and copy the second commandment onto your big red heart. Teach your child that this commandment is helping us understand *how* to worship God.

4. Turn to 1 Kings 8:10–11. Read or tell your child the story of the dedication of King Solomon's temple. Then turn to 2 Kings 21:1–9 and 24:1–3 and explain how certain kings wanted to worship in God's temple but bring in their own ways of doing so. What was the Lord's response?

5. Help your child understand that how we worship God is very important to him because it shows him whom we love. Talk about attitudes and behaviors during public and family worship time. Help him to see that God is seeking true worshipers (John 4:23–24; Hebrews 12:28–29). Does your child see you as a passionate lover of God?

6. Talk together about images of God. You may have a pictorial Bible. Explain why a picture could never show the real God we worship (refer to Exodus 33:12–23). Describe a friend or relative whom your child has never met, and ask him to draw a picture of that person. Then show him that person's picture. Compare and discuss.

7. Ask your child if people have to see something in order for it to be real. Blow up one balloon, then talk about the fact that even though we can't see air, it is very powerful (mention wind, storms, and even our breath, which sustains life). Air can even make noise—pop the balloon!

8. Blow up the second balloon, and then talk about how we like to make God into something we can see and touch. Explain to your child that just as the air in the balloon is such a teeny-tiny part of all the air in the

world, so is any picture or image of God we try to make. Just like air, God cannot be contained. Leave your blown-up balloon around the house for a few days and draw attention to it as the air slowly leaks out.

9. Tape the third balloon near the second commandment on your big red heart to remind your child that God can never be contained or confined to any human representation.

CHAPTER THREE

EVERYTHING IN THE NAME OF THE LORD JESUS

"You shall not take the name of the Lord *your God in vain, for the* Lord *will not hold him guiltless who takes his name in vain."*

EXODUS 20:7

HIS LOVING LAW

What's in a Name?

To understand the third commandment we must understand why God takes his name so seriously. Today a name is little more than a personal label. My husband, Ray, would be just as insightful and tenderhearted if he were John or Charlie or Bubba. Actually, his family calls him Bud. But in the Bible, a name often goes much deeper than a simple label. Think of how particular God was at times to name certain people—Abraham, Sarah, Isaac (Genesis 17:5, 15, 19), Jacob renamed as Israel (Genesis 32:28), and, of course, Jesus (Matthew 21:1).

The giving of a name was the prerogative of a superior—a parent or a king or a chief. Joseph's name was changed by Pharaoh

(Genesis 41:45) and Daniel's by the chief of Nebuchadnezzar's eunuchs (Daniel 1:7).

A name would match the character or function of a person. Moses named his son born to him in Midian, Gershom, which sounds like the Hebrew for *sojourner* and means "resident alien" (Exodus 2:22). Sometimes the selection of a name signified hope. Think of Jacob's wives, Leah and Rachel. Leah felt Jacob's scorn and named her sons accordingly (Genesis 29:32–35). And Joseph, one of Rachel's sons, means "may he add" and sounds like the Hebrew word for *taken away*. Rachel felt that her reproach had been taken away, and she was already hoping for another son.

One other function of naming someone must be understood to grasp the meaning of this commandment. Whenever the name bearer placed his own name upon another, it signified the joining of two separate persons in the closest of unions.[1] We see this in a husband giving his name to his wife (Isaiah 4:1), or in Israel being called by Yahweh's name (Deuteronomy 28:9–10). And in the New Testament, believers are baptized "into" (*eis* with the accusative) *the name* of the Father and of the Son and of the Holy Spirit (Matthew 28:19). This union signifies a new ownership, a deep loyalty, and a rich fellowship.

God's Name Is His Person, Character, and Reputation Revealed

In Leviticus 24:10–16, the son of an Israelite woman and Egyptian father was sentenced to death because he blasphemed the Name. This had to be more than a mere slip of the tongue. This was so grievous to God that it bore the ultimate punishment. God's name is more than a label. Where his name is implicated, he is personally involved and will take action.

His name is his *self-revelation*, what he wants us to know about himself. He has revealed his name as a refuge: "The name of the Lord is a strong tower; the righteous man runs into it and is safe" (Proverbs 18:10). Today, we would not say we run into a name for safety. He has revealed his name as active: "The name of the LORD comes from afar, burning with his anger, and in thick rising smoke . . ." (Isaiah 30:27). His name is linked with:

- goodness (Psalm 100:4, 5);
- mercy (Psalm 109:21);
- righteousness (Psalm 89:15, 16);
- faithfulness and steadfast love (Psalm 89:24);
- salvation (Psalm 96:2); and
- holiness (Psalm 99:3).

His name can be:

- despised (Isaiah 52:5); and
- profaned or defiled (Jeremiah 34:16; Proverbs 30:9).

His name can also be:

- loved (Psalm 5:11);
- praised (Joel 2:26);
- walked in (Micah 4:5);
- esteemed (Malachi 3:16);
- waited on (Psalm 52:9);
- given thanks to (Psalm 54:6);
- feared (Malachi 4:2);
- called upon (Psalm 99:6); and
- blessed (Psalm 145:1, 2).

We see throughout Scripture that God's name signifies *his revealed character and his esteemed reputation*:

- "He leads me in paths of righteousness *for his name's sake*" (Psalm 23:3).

- "*For your name's sake*, O LORD, pardon my guilt" (Psalm 25:11).
- "Help us, O God of our salvation, for the glory of your name; deliver us, and atone for our sins, *for your name's sake*! Why should the nations say, 'Where is their God?'" (Psalm 79:9–10).
- "Though our iniquities testify against us, act, O LORD, for *your name's sake*; for our backslidings are many . . . we are called by your name; do not leave us" (Jeremiah 14:7–9).
- "But I had concern for my holy name, which the house of Israel had profaned among the nations to which they came. . . . It is not for your sake, O house of Israel, that I am about to act, *but for the sake of my holy name*, which you have profaned among the nations . . . And I will vindicate the holiness of my great name. . . . And the nations will know that I am the LORD . . ." (Ezekiel 36:21–23).

God's Active Presence in His Name

When Elijah challenged the prophets of Baal and Asherah to a contest to see which god was the true God, he proposed a contest between the names of their respective gods. 1 Kings 18:24 says, "You call upon the name of your god, and I will call upon the name of the LORD, and the God who answers by fire, he is God." The name of God signifies the active presence of his person in his revealed character.

When his name is upon a people, they are blessed. Think of Aaron's blessing in Numbers 6:24–26, often used as a blessing at baptisms or as a benediction:

> The LORD bless you and keep you;
> the LORD make his face to shine upon you and be gracious to you;
> the LORD lift up his countenance upon you and give you peace.

Have you ever noticed the surrounding verses? "The LORD spoke to Moses. . . . 'Thus you shall bless the people'" (vv. 22–23). And verse 27 reads, "So shall they *put my name* upon the people of Israel and I will bless them."

To bless someone is to put God's name upon them. You are offering a prayer that the one blessed may know the active presence of God in the fullness of his revealed character. Think of how many times God's name has been put upon you in blessing and benediction of favor and grace and protection and peace.

I have decided to say good-bye to each of our grandchildren after our visits with this prayer from Numbers 6. May God's active presence surround them in ways only he can during our separations from each other. Where God's name is, there is blessing, because where his name is, he is being revealed. "In every place where I cause my name to be remembered I will come to you and bless you" (Exodus 20:24).

How God Loves Us through This Commandment

God loves us in this commandment by revealing himself to us through his name. His names are packed with doctrinal content. They are affirmations of our faith. Think of what his names teach us about himself:

- He is the God who sees (Genesis 16:13; Jeremiah 32:19).
- He is Elohim, the omnipotent creator (Isaiah 40:25–26, 28).
- He is El Shaddai, the sovereign Lord, or God Almighty, the all-sufficient one (Genesis 17:1).
- He is El-Elohe-Israel, the God of Israel (Genesis 33:20).
- He is LORD, Yahweh (Jehovah), God's personal name, which expresses the essence of God's character. He is the self-existent, self-sufficient Sovereign who depends on no one (Exodus 3:13–14; Isaiah 43:10–13, 15).
- He is Jehovah-Rapha, the Lord who heals (Psalm 103:1–3).
- He is Jehovah-Nissi, "the LORD is my banner," our security in the presence of our enemies (Exodus 17:15).
- He is Jehovah-Jireh, the one who will provide (Genesis 22:14).
- He is Jehovah-Shalom, "The LORD is Peace" (Judges 6:24).

His names teach us about him. They show us how he relates to his people. Each name is an affirmation of faith. When I esteem

God's peace, providence, righteousness, sovereignty, and holiness, I am reverencing God.

He Tells Us What Would Dishonor His Name

God tells us that we may not treat his name lightly. The word translated "vain" connotes something thin and pale and worthless and empty. It means *nothingness*. How do we take God's name in vain? How do we misuse it? We misuse it when we treat God's name as if it were nothingness. God loves us by telling us how not to dishonor his name. He cares how we treat his name, because we are in a love relationship.

We Take His Name in Vain with Our Words

As our cultural communication takes on more and more vulgarity, we see God's name mentioned frequently in casual, meaningless chatter. But the third commandment tells us this is wrong—it shows contempt for God and cheapens his name.

I have a confession: I'm a "Wheel Watcher." If I am home at 6:30 of an evening I'll try to convince Ray to watch *Wheel of Fortune* with me (he is so long-suffering with all my foibles). But some nights I turn it off. Why? Because sometimes God's name is bandied about so carelessly by contestants. When we say, "Oh my God!" or "Good Lord!" or even "Lord, have mercy!" when we win some huge prize, or stub our toe, or get cut off in the carpool line, we are taking God's name in vain. We must not blaspheme God. Ever. Period.

The way we verbally reference another person has a profound effect on how we regard and treat that person. The same holds true in our regard for God. "People who have turned their backs on God naturally take up using his name idly."[2]

Do we simply shrug our shoulders at the cursing of another or do we see her words exposing her deepest emptiness? Would we use a friend's or husband's name as flippantly as some use God's holy name? Words display our unseen souls. "For out of the overflow of the heart the mouth speaks" (Matthew 12:34 NIV).

I have taught second grade for thirteen years, twelve of them in public schools. One fall during teacher training we had a speaker who, though very insightful and extremely funny, repeatedly used God's name to punctuate his points. I found myself growing more and more uncomfortable as the training session went on. Later over lunch, my coworkers were discussing how much they enjoyed his presentation and asked me what I thought of it. They were shocked when I told them it was difficult for me to listen because of all the times he used God's name flippantly. "Is it hard for you when we say, 'O God!'?" my closest teammate asked. When I shared with them my convictions, I was humbled at their response—apologies and honest efforts at change when they were with me. How kind of them.

There are other more subtle ways to take his name in vain. We make light of his name when we add it to lend force to our language. Often this springs from good intentions. "The Lord led me to tell you . . ." "I believe it is God's will that you . . ." Or, "I swear, with God as my witness . . ." (Isn't your word alone enough?) Religious jargon violates the third commandment.

We also take God's name in vain when we worship him with our lips but not with our hearts (see Isaiah 29:13). "My son, give me your heart" (Proverbs 23:26). Dead, externalized worship violates the third commandment.

Finally, we take his name in vain when we murmur or complain against him, which is to speak evil of him (Exodus 16:7–8; Numbers 14:26). "They say to God, 'Depart from us! We do not desire the knowledge of your ways. What is the Almighty, that we should serve him? And what profit do we get if we pray to him?'" (Job 21:14–15).

We Take His Name in Vain in Our Actions

The third commandment targets so much more than how we speak about God. I could go through life and never let a bad word slip out of my mouth and still break this commandment. How? By professing his name but not living by it. Whenever my life does not bear out what my words say, I am breaking this commandment. "They profess to know God, but they deny him by their works" (Titus 1:16). We deny God's self-revelation, taking his name in vain, when we bear his name but do not live in the fullness of who he is. We are treating his name as nothingness when we call ourselves Christians, but to us he's unreal—nothing.

Whenever we settle into a dull, empty Christian experience, with no struggle, no pressing on, as if Jesus were boring, yet we call ourselves Christians, we are taking up his name as nothingness—in vain. God has revealed himself to us as I AM WHO I AM (Exodus 3:14). He is absolute, eternal, unchangeable, ultimate, delightful, all-satisfying reality. To identify myself with him—to call myself a Christian—but not to live as if all that his name means really matters, is to take his name in vain. A bored, self-centered Christian following a glorious God takes his name in vain! And where does this leave every one of us but humbled to our knees?

OUR LASTING LEGACY

Living the Third Commandment

The positive side of the third commandment is found in the first phrase of the Lord's Prayer: "Hallowed be your name" (Matthew 6:9). When we hallow his name, we:

- treat it as holy, separate, and above every other name in the universe;
- hold it in reverence;
- stand in awe of it; and
- recognize it as sacred.

When we hallow his name, we guard our hearts and ears against becoming desensitized to the desecration of his holy name.

If you call yourself a Christian, you have the name of the God of the universe upon you. And it is a costly name. God sacrificed his Son to adopt you into his family and give you his name. Does your life bear a family resemblance to your first-born Brother? Let us be women who sense his holy presence and hallow his name in our lives by living like we're really his! I wonder if anyone can tell I am a Christian before I ever open my mouth?

Giving the Third Commandment

In the midst of a cultural ideal that marginalizes and trivializes God, trying to make him look small, let's learn how to honor God for his greatness. Let us be women who savor and love and serve him, and call our children to savor and love and serve him. Let's not let the world hover too close to our heart.

The third commandment encourages us to live as though God is everything he reveals himself to be, to treat God as everything that in fact he is! If you want more of the living God than you have ever had before, the third commandment is assuring you that that's what God wants too. God is saying to his children, "All that I am I want to put on you as you bear my name."

Come to God. Tell him, "Your name is holy. Now help me to live like it is. Teach me how to better honor your name in my words and deeds. Let me live a life of holy reverence because I bear your name." As you seek to bear God's name, meditate on these verses:

> Our help is in the *name* of the LORD,
> who made heaven and earth. (Psalm 124:8)

> Bless the LORD, O my soul,
> and all that is within me bless his holy *name*! (Psalm 103:1)

> Your *name* and remembrance are the desire of our soul. (Isaiah 26:8)

> In every place where I cause my *name* to be remembered I will come to you and bless you. (Exodus 20:24)

> Not to us, O LORD, not to us, but to your *name* give glory,
> for the sake of your steadfast love and your faithfulness! (Psalm 115:1)

> Ascribe to the Lord the glory due his *name*. (Psalm 96:8)

> Fear this glorious and awesome *name*. (Deuteronomy 28:58)

> But to all who did receive him, who believed in his *name*, he gave the right to become children of God. (John 1:12)

> But these are written so that you may believe that Jesus is the Christ, the Son of God, and that by believing you may have life in his *name*. (John 20:31)

> Oh, magnify the Lord with me,
> and let us exalt his *name* together! (Psalm 34:3)

We sometimes struggle to honor God's name the way we should; we take it in vain. But someday we will take God's name on ourselves perfectly. We will worship God as real and weighty and glorious and valuable and near. Never again will God be blasphemed or ignored or forgotten or belittled:

> All the nations you have made shall come
> and worship before you, O Lord,
> and shall glorify your *name*. (Psalm 86:9)

> So that at the *name* of Jesus every knee should bow, in heaven and on earth and under the earth, and every tongue confess that Jesus Christ is Lord, to the glory of God the Father. (Philippians 2:10–11)

> The Lord will be king over all the earth. On that day there will be one Lord, and his *name* the only name. (Zechariah 14:9 niv)

Let's live a life of holy reverence before watching eyes and listening ears, giving this command to the next generation.

Everything in the Name of the Lord Jesus

STUDY AND DISCUSSION FOR LIVING THE THIRD COMMANDMENT

1. Memorize the first three commandments. Review Psalm 119:18.

2. Think about your own name. Does it have any special significance?

3. Have you, or anyone you love, ever been slandered? Describe the situation and your response.

4. Study the following verses with this question in mind: What does God's name "I AM" teach you about him?

   - Exodus 3:13–14
   - Exodus 6:3
   - Isaiah 43:10–13, 15

5. What do we learn about the holiness of God's name from Ezekiel 36:16–32?

6. Meditate on Psalm 103:1 and Colossians 3:17. Write these verses out and put them where you will see them each day—maybe near your kitchen sink or on your bathroom mirror. Think about how often we take God's name in vain by cursing or idle chatter or religious jargon or spiritual indifference. Ask God to give you one new way to honor his holy name this week.

7. Read Isaiah 26:8. How can you hallow God's name in:

   - your heart
   - your home

- your church
- your worship (both public and private)
- your community

8. Spend some time exalting and magnifying God's name as you think through these verses:

    - Numbers 6:24–27
    - Psalm 23:3
    - Psalm 124:8
    - Proverbs 18:10
    - Jeremiah 14:7–9
    - Zechariah 14:9
    - Philippians 2:9–11

STUDY AND DISCUSSION FOR GIVING THE THIRD COMMANDMENT TO OUR CHILDREN

Materials needed: Bible, marker, index card, pencil, tape, the big red heart, and a copy of *Prince Caspian* by C. S. Lewis (optional).

1. Review the first two commandments with your child and then read Exodus 20:7. Memorize the third commandment together.

2. Talk with your child about family names—yours, your child's, your parents'—and discuss the significance of each name.

3. Spend some time talking with your child about what it means to be part of a family. Those who bear the same name need to stick up for each other. Teach your child how his actions reflect on the family name. Work this week on building more of a family brotherhood. This should influence how family members treat each other, support each other, and talk about each other.

4. Talk about how a name can be misused, perhaps with teasing. How does that make a person feel? What can you do to help defend someone's name? Model for your child how other people's names are safe in your house. Don't let gossip and slander travel around your kitchen table or through your phones.

5. Write the third commandment on your big red heart.

6. Have your kids heard God's name taken in vain on TV? In books? In movies? From other kids? In your home? Talk to your child about what it means to take God's name in vain and how to honor his name.

7. Read Isaiah 26:8 and Colossians 3:17 with your child. Think together about ways you can honor God's reputation in your home and family life, both in words and in deeds. Throughout the week look for ways your family hallows God's name in actions and words. Record them on an index card and tape the card next to the third commandment on the big red heart.

8. One of the ways to tell if your child is growing in Christ is if his esteem of and delight in God are expanding. God will keep growing bigger to him! C. S. Lewis captures this idea perfectly in chapter 10 of *Prince Caspian*, one of the books in his series *The Chronicles of Narnia*. Don't miss this. Make a plan to read it with your child and then discuss it.

CHAPTER FOUR

NEXT REST STOP: SUNDAY

"Remember the Sabbath day, to keep it holy."

EXODUS 20:8

Before we begin our discussion of the fourth commandment, it will be helpful to think about the purposes of the law in the Old Testament and how the law relates to us today. Why are the Ten Commandments still honored by New Testament believers when other laws in the Old Testament are not? How are we to understand the various laws in the Old Testament?

There were three kinds of law in Old Testament times. One kind is the *moral* law, which is the righteous standard for our relationship with God and others. It is a permanent obligation, written by God (Exodus 32:16), and the only part of the law kept in the ark of the covenant (Exodus 25:16). The moral law is the foundation of all other laws and is eternal in its nature and function.

The second kind, *civil*, or *judicial* law, consisted of laws for Israel as a nation. God intended Israel to be a theocracy and represent him in her reign of peace and righteousness on earth. These laws dealt with war, land use, debt, and other laws concerning Israel as a nation. They pointed forward to the kingdom of Christ and foreshadowed Christ as king.

The third kind, *ceremonial* law, told the Israelites how to conduct worship in the sanctuary and during festivals. These laws gave instructions for the sacrificial system. They pointed forward to the cross and foreshadowed Christ as prophet and priest.

Both the ceremonial and civil laws contained shadows of the real and lasting things God meant to give us all along. When Christ came, there was no longer any need for the shadows. Now that Christ has come, these laws have been set aside because the substance belongs to Christ, who is "the true form of these realities" (Hebrews 10:1; Colossians 2:17).

The fourth commandment is the only one of the Ten Commandments about which interpretation has been hotly debated throughout the centuries. Every single one of the Ten Commandments is repeated in the New Testament except the fourth commandment. I believe that the Lord's Day, or the first day of the week (Acts 20:7; 1 Corinthians 16:2; Revelation 1:10) is the New Testament fulfillment of the Old Testament Sabbath, and as God's redeemed we are to keep this command just as we are to hallow his name and to worship him the way he tells us to.

HIS LOVING LAW

What if you were driving down the interstate on a long road trip and you saw a sign:

NEXT REST STOP: NOWHERE

How discouraging that would be! And sometimes we feel that our lives are like that—always on the road, never able to pull off for a short break. But God has put his own road sign along our highway to heaven:

NEXT REST STOP: SUNDAY

Think if someone told you there was a way to glorify and enjoy God, step out of your overcommitted pace of life, slow down enough to catch your breath and refresh your soul, revive relationships with family and friends, think about the most worthy things in life, and share your blessings with those in need—all by obeying the fourth commandment. You would say that's impossible! But it isn't. Listen to how God loves us through this law.

He Liberates Us

The fourth commandment refers to creation. "For in six days the Lord made heaven and earth, the sea, and all that is in them, and rested on the seventh day" (Exodus 20:11). In six days God made it all, but on the seventh he rested. Now God didn't have to rest. He is never depleted. But it was his delight to rest, and he blessed the pattern. "God blessed the seventh day and made it holy" (Genesis 2:3). In Exodus 31:17 we read, "It is a sign forever between me and the people of Israel that in six days the Lord made heaven and earth, and on the seventh day he rested and was refreshed."

He not only rests, but he also calls us to rest with him and to call others within our spheres of influence to rest, as well. The Sabbath is God's *gift* to us. Even before the Ten Commandments were given, the people of Israel knew that the Lord had given them the Sabbath (Exodus 16:29–30).

Jesus tells us in Mark 2:27, "The Sabbath was made for man, not man for the Sabbath." Man was created on the sixth day; he already existed when God made the Sabbath on the seventh day (Genesis 2:1–3). God loves us by creating a universal pattern where we lay down our pride and accept his offer of rest. God's gift to us is one-seventh of our time, freed from the cares and labors of our work, to spend loving and enjoying him and others. One day out of each week—fifty-two days a year—is nearly seven and a half weeks of rest each year!

We are God's servants, and he calls us to rest. "You shall remember that you were a slave in the land of Egypt, and the Lord your God brought you out from there. . . . Therefore the Lord your God commanded you to keep the Sabbath day" (Deuteronomy 5:15).

The Sabbath is a day of remembering our liberation. Think of what a day of rest meant for a slave. A slave never had a day off!

God wants to free us from thinking that our jobs provide for us. They don't; *he* does. God loves us by providing for seven days' worth of needs through only six days of work. He wants us to trust him to make up the difference.

He Exposes Our Sin

God loves us in the fourth commandment by showing us our natural bent toward pride. Are you thinking, "God wants *how* much of my time? Seven weeks each year? Doesn't he know how busy I am carrying out all the responsibilities he has given me?" Why does this gift make us so uncomfortable?

We have developed a God-neglecting, soul-starving pace of life, bearing the weight of the world on our shoulders. Our compulsive self-efforts show that we are afraid to rest. It is a form of pride, of self-dependence. Think of all our over-scheduled Sundays. We still go to church, but somehow we squeeze it in between sporting events, chores, and shopping sprees.

This commandment comes along and shows us our sin. It says that an all-consuming pace of life is not God's will for us. He loves us by calling us to a weekly rhythm of six days of work broken by a day of holy rest.

He Gives Us Newness of Life

God loves us by giving us one day each week that is set above the ordinary routine of everyday life. Here is a day set aside for the purpose of coming to God anew in worship and delight and beauty. We enter into what God has already done. And it goes on into eternity. Have you noticed how all six days of the creation account in Genesis 1 conclude with, "So there was evening and morning, the ____ day"? But when Moses narrates the seventh day, it is not brought to closure. The text of Genesis 2:1–3 does not say, "And there was evening and there was morning the seventh day."

The day of rest and holy blessing stands open. It points to heaven. Our enjoyment and delight in the Lord's Day—or lack thereof—reveals how earthbound we are, because each Sunday is a little rehearsal for heaven where we will enter a Sabbath rest that God has prepared for us. "There remains a Sabbath rest for the people of God. . . . Let us therefore strive to enter that rest" (Hebrews 4:9, 11). God loves us in this commandment by showing us that real life is not down here, but out there with him, in an eternity of true worship and soul rest.

OUR LASTING LEGACY

Living the Fourth Commandment

Let his day be one of delight. By the time of Christ, the fourth commandment had been so mistreated and misrepresented that the Sabbath had become a day of don'ts rather than a day of delights. For example:

- A radish could be dipped in salt, but not for too long because that could begin the pickling process.
- A woman was forbidden to look in the glass on the Sabbath because she might discover a white hair and pull it out, which would be a sin.
- Parents were allowed to pick up their child, but not if he was carrying anything, because then they would be lifting a burden.
- To pick up a piece of fruit from the ground was reaping and, therefore, sin.
- If a woman spilled on her dress, it was debated whether she should shake it off or wring it dry.[1]

There was no discussion of anything spiritual, nothing to suggest a glad celebration of God's gift to us of a whole day of worship and rest. This was a heavy, endless list of burdensome rules. The day of holy delights had become a day of don'ts. Rules make the day of the Spirit unspiritual. They hinder our spirits.

But one can err on the other side. Back in Isaiah's day, people were ignoring the Sabbath for the sake of business. They had no time to fit God into their busy weeks (Isaiah 58). God comes to us in the fourth commandment and lovingly shows us there is more to life than work. God says it is to be a day of liberation (Isaiah 58:6), kindness (Isaiah 58:7), and holy delight (Isaiah 58:14).

Don't rob God of his day. God tells us that we can work during six days, but one out of every seven is for his and our use alone. He calls us to stop the everyday treadmill that we have jumped on. We tend to work ourselves to death. Solomon taught, "It is in vain that you rise up early and go late to rest, eating the bread of anxious toil" (Psalm 127:2). Work shouldn't control us. We should control our work.

How can we liberate this day, making it one of kindness and holy delight? Well, surely not by creating another set of rules. We must never add to what the Bible says. Let's not use Sunday to oppress our family by setting up such strict guidelines that our children come to Sunday with little anticipation, and perhaps even resentment. The Lord has told us that he is Lord of the Sabbath, that this is his day (Mark 2:28). Whose day? The Lord's. But whose benefit? Ours! We're not slaves anymore. This day is God's good gift to us. Let's use it to liberate enslaved souls.

How can we make this day a delight? Only when our deepest joy is in God will his day become our day of delight. If God is burdensome, then his day will be burdensome as well. When our worship loses reality with God, it becomes perfunctory, and then we marginalize it because it becomes a burden rather than a joy. This command, like the three preceding ones, is really a matter of the heart (Deuteronomy 32:46–47). Is God a burden to us?

God is reminding us that our main purpose in life is to enjoy him, to worship him. And meaningful worship in the manifest presence of the King of the universe is so deeply satisfying that it will become our delight to participate in worship. We will hardly be able to wait for Sunday to roll around. "I was glad when they said to me, 'Let us go to the house of the LORD!'" (Psalm 122:1).

Let's dedicate this day. Jesus did not come to destroy this commandment, but to fulfill it (Matthew 5:17). He does so by calling us to himself alone on the Lord's Day to the exclusion of our ordinary duties and preoccupations. My Ray puts it this way: "Jesus invites us harried, breathless, modern people to slow down and for one whole day do nothing but indulge ourselves in his goodness and truth."

God has given us a loving rhythm of six days of work broken with a day of holy rest. How can you dedicate this day to him and draw refreshment from his invitation to rest in an atmosphere of holy delight? Ask God to help you make his day special. He will show you how. Wrestle with this commandment. It will look different for each one of us.

I find the key to dedication in the first word of this command—"Remember." Let's not leave this day to chance. You plan your other six days. Why not take even more care to plan the Lord's Day? If you were devoting a whole day to someone else—a loved one or spouse or friend—what would it look like? Or what if someone said, "I want to devote next Saturday to you. What would you like me to do? How can I please you and show you what you mean to me?" What would God have your Sundays look like? Ask God to help you make his day special. He will show you how. Search the Word, pray, discuss this with family and friends, and make changes.

Certainly such plans would include corporate worship with other believers. Leviticus 23:3 calls the Sabbath "a holy convocation." So it would be a day given over to God, set apart for him and for his glory. This would include gathering with others for worship. And we wouldn't just give God an hour and ten minutes, rushing in and rushing out so we can make it to the game or the beach or the mall. We would prepare ourselves. But preparation takes dedication. What do your Saturdays look like? Do you crash all day Saturday, waking up late Sunday with a rushed mental list of things to do before Monday with church tagged on somewhere between stopping at the drugstore and going to the football game?

Sunday is the Lord's Day. How would he want us to spend it? Do we give our best energies for playing and entertaining and amusements on Saturday night and then come to church tired and listless and late? Is our worship perfunctory? Do we live out this commandment by going to church and then doing the "fun stuff"?

To dedicate ourselves to this day of delights will take planning. It will mean saying no to certain invitations on Saturday. It will mean thinking through the day ahead.

Giving the Fourth Commandment

The coming generations need to see the delight of a Sabbath rest this side of heaven. And they need to see it from us. They need to see that this is a "get to" not a "got to."

We lived in Scotland for four years while Ray earned his PhD from the University of Aberdeen. Ray assisted at our parish church and left home early on Sunday mornings. It was hard for me to get the kids ready and willing for our mile walk to and from church (we had no car at the time). So I decided to try to make Sunday morning the best morning of the week. We made yeast dough on Saturday and rolled out several cinnamon rolls to sit rising overnight. The children would wake up to that wonderful aroma, which still brings us back in our hearts to our tiny kitchen there along Royal Deeside.

I made sure their clothes were ready to put on without the needless frictions of "I can't find my other shoe!" and "This shirt is dirty!" and "Have you seen my jacket?" And then after a special breakfast we would set out, me with "sweeties" in my pocket to award cheerful conversation and quick obedience. On the way we would talk about what a special hour was before us, the one hour of the week where we could worship God together with our friends, and how Mummy needed her children to sit very quietly for just this one hour so she could listen and pray and sing and give and celebrate the sacraments (there was no nursery the first two years we lived in Scotland). I encouraged them to try to join in as they were able.

Then we would get the wiggles out on the way home with happy words about our worship and fellowship, and many thanks from me for how they had loved me and honored Jesus and respected the adults around them with their quiet bodies and mouths.

To this day we still have a special sit-down breakfast on Sunday mornings whenever the kids are home. We love Sunday mornings. But what about the rest of the day? How can we make Sundays different, delightfully different? We can learn to get our work done in six days. We can follow God's example. Why does this seem like a punishment rather than a delight? Why does this make us resentful? Because we love to carry our own burdens and lift them high to validate our worth with our incessant rounds of busyness.

Somehow my washer seems to call to me on Sunday afternoons. Does yours? My friend Anne has four active boys and one beautiful daughter, plus a continual flow of students who need housing, along with visiting missionaries and frequent houseguests. Her laundry room is always full of socks and sweats and shirts and sheets. She told me that once after hearing a man preach on the fourth commandment, she asked him, "Is it all right for me to do laundry on Sunday?" He answered, "Why would you *want* to do laundry on Sunday?" Indeed.

We follow God by working hard for six days and then resting. As we examined earlier, God not only rests, but he calls us to rest with him. God structures our calendar for our blessing. And he instructs us to call others within our spheres of influence into that blessing (Exodus 20:9–10).

Years ago we encouraged our children to get their homework done on Saturday so they could really enjoy the Lord's Day. Still today we don't pay bills or clean the house or do our taxes or finish up that big pile of ironing. And we rejoice in that. What a blessing to have a day that is different from all the rest!

We have needs all seven days of the week, and emergencies do arise. But God wants to provide seven days' worth of needs through only six days of labor. Learn to trust God to make up the difference. God wants us to lift up our heads from our deadlines and shopping lists and laundry and to look at him.

God is calling us to leave a margin in our lives so that we can see how much he cares for and loves us. It bears repeating that God wants to protect and nurture us by giving us a day that is different from the other six each week, a day where we can savor the sweetness of life with him. The word *Sabbath* comes from the Hebrew word meaning "to cease or to rest." It is a day to step back from the onslaught of everyday obligations in order to refresh ourselves in God's goodness and grace. Thomas Watson said, "God made this day on purpose to raise the heart to heaven, to converse with him, to do angel's work."[2]

This is a day for worship and rest, but also for deeds of mercy. Real needs must be met on the Sabbath. We find Sunday a wonderful time for visiting the "sick and sorrowing" when our workweeks are too full. There are always people around us in need. This is a perfect day to "Share with God's people who are in need. Practice hospitality." (Romans 12:13 NIV).

This is not just a "family day"; it is the Lord's Day. It is a day to walk, talk, read, rest, play games, visit neighbors or shut-ins. When God gave us the Sabbath, he meant it as a blessing for man—a gift for us, not simply a formal observance.

How will you live and give this day to those around you? How will you delight in it, plan for it, and differentiate it from every other day of the week? How will you live out this wonderful gift and give it to your children?

STUDY AND DISCUSSION FOR LIVING THE FOURTH COMMANDMENT

1. How is your memory work coming along? Try writing your verses on index cards and keeping them near you for easy reference. Review Psalm 119:18 and the first three commandments. Now work on memorizing the fourth commandment and Deuteronomy 32:46–47.

2. Carefully read these verses, jotting down your observations about the Sabbath:

   - Genesis 2:1–3
   - Exodus 16:29–30
   - Exodus 20:11
   - Exodus 31:16–17
   - Hebrews 4:9–13

3. What kind of day is the Sabbath meant to be? Read Isaiah 58:9–14. Can you state both the positive and negative of this commandment?

4. What do your Sundays look like? Read Exodus 20:9–10. What new steps can you take to make the Lord's Day a day of delight for everyone in your circle of life?

STUDY AND DISCUSSION FOR GIVING THE FOURTH COMMANDMENT TO OUR CHILDREN

Materials needed: markers, Bible, index cards, dictionary, tape, and the big red heart.

1. Review with your child the first three commandments. Read together the fourth commandment and print it on the big red heart. Discuss how your family presently spends Sundays. Listen to what your child likes and dislikes about the family routine.

2. Read together Genesis 2:1–3 and Exodus 31:16–17. Discuss the whole idea of the Sabbath with your child. Talk about who made it and why. Ask, does God ever get tired? Look up the word *covenant* in the dictionary and write out a definition together in your own words (the word *covenant* is mentioned almost three hundred times in Scripture).

3. Read Mark 2:23–3:6. Talk together about what Jesus did on the Sabbath and what he taught about it.

4. Discuss with your child why we "honor the Sabbath" on Sunday. See Matthew 28:1–7, Mark 16:1–7, Luke 24:1–8, and John 20:1.

5. Look together at what things the New Testament church did on Sundays (first called the Lord's Day in Revelation 1:10). See Acts 20:7 and 1 Corinthians 16:2.

6. Discuss with your child how you make certain days special in your family (i.e., birthdays, holidays, last day of school, graduations). Help your child to see how Sunday is a special day. Think of one new way your family can make Sunday more delightful. Draw a small picture of this new idea and tape it onto the big red heart near the fourth commandment. Pray about it and put it into practice this next Lord's Day. Afterwards, talk about how it went.

CHAPTER FIVE

IT ALL BEGINS AT HOME

"Honor your father and your mother, that your days may be long in the land that the Lord *your God is giving you."*

EXODUS 20:12

We now begin the second part of the Decalogue, another name for the Ten Commandments. In the first four commandments God lovingly instructs us on how to respond to his redemptive love. We are to love the Lord above all else and with all our capacities (Matthew 22:34–40). With God, relationship precedes requirement. The next six commandments teach us how to love our neighbors as ourselves.

We have seen that first came the gospel of liberation: "I am the Lord your God who brought you out of the . . . house of slavery" (Exodus 20:2). Now come God's loving instructions for staying free, and the very first one begins in the home with the parent-child relationship. How very important this must be to God.

HIS LOVING LAW

The Flow of Human Relationships

The fifth commandment is about the flow of human relationships, and at the very center of all relations is that between parent and child. God loves us in this command by showing us how to live together in close family units, which will, in turn, affect every relationship outside the home.

God's desire is to preserve the intergenerational continuance of a vibrant faith in God. A child's whole life is shaped by his parents. They are the ones who interpret reality to their child. Parents are the ones who can teach their children day by day to see God and to savor God.

What *Honor* Means

The word *honor* comes from a Hebrew word meaning "to be heavy" or "to give weight." It involves taking someone seriously into account, offering that person profound respect and a place of importance and reverence. The opposite of honoring someone is trivializing him, despising him, forgetting him, or treating him as if he didn't matter.

Loving, honoring, and respecting others starts at home. The family is the first and primary set of relationships and the beginning of all human society. "Father and mother" in this command most certainly mean our natural parents, those typically nearest and dearest to us. And this is the main emphasis of the fifth commandment. The implications, however, are far ranging. What child who loves and honors his parents disrespects authority outside his home? The respect a child learns for authority in his home (or the lack thereof) bears far-reaching effects into his school, his neighborhood, his church, his city, his country, and his world.

Whom We Should Honor

Remember that a commandment requires obedience to the command, not only to its exact wording, but also to all it implies. For instance, "You shall not commit adultery" means also that you are not to flirt. And "You shall not kill" includes not hating someone. So, too, with this commandment. The Bible teaches various areas where we are required to show respect.

- In our communities:

> Be subject for the Lord's sake to every human institution. (1 Peter 2:13)

> Let every person be subject to the governing authorities. For there is no authority except from God, and those that exist have been instituted by God. (Romans 13:1)

- In our churches:

> Shepherd the flock of God that is among you, exercising oversight, not under compulsion, but willingly . . . eagerly . . . not domineering over those in your charge, but being examples. . . . Likewise, you who are younger, be subject to the elders. (1 Peter 5:2–5)

> Obey your leaders and submit to them, for they are keeping watch over your souls, as those who will have to give an account. Let them do this with joy and not with groaning, for that would be of no advantage to you. (Hebrews 13:17)

- In our homes:

> Listen to your father who gave you life, and do not despise your mother when she is old. (Proverbs 23:22)

> Hear, O sons, a father's instruction, and be attentive, that you may gain insight. (Proverbs 4:1)

I believe this key issue of respect begins in our homes, and particularly with us as women. There were four kids in my family when I was growing up, two boys and two girls. My little sister must have been three or four years old when she decided that she had had enough of this having-to-obey-Mommy stuff! I remember Mom reining her in on something one night at dinner, and Pati declaring with all the defiance she could muster, "Well then, I just won't love you anymore!" My five-year-old mind had never witnessed so brash a statement, and I felt sure my little sis had scored a big one on softening Mom's resolve, because I knew even then how very much Mom adored us kids.

But Mom's response was one I'll never forget. It shaped the whole tenor of our home life and she enforced it through the years. She stood up to her full 5-feet, 4-inch frame, looked little Pati straight in the eye and said, "You do not have to love me, but you must respect me. Now do as I said." The discussion was ended!

I believe women are key in this issue of respect. If children learn respect in their homes, then they will be able to respect other people in authority. When I was teaching, I never found a child to be disrespectful to me and to other school authorities if his mother required respect at home. If children honor their parents, they will honor their teachers, their church leaders, their community and leaders—all of society benefits.

OUR LASTING LEGACY

Living the Fifth Commandment

Living the fifth commandment means modeling respect. As you live your calling as wife, daughter, mother, grandmother, sister, aunt, church member, and citizen, are the children in your life seeing you model respect for those in authority over you? How do they hear you speak to their father? What do they hear you say about your parents and your in-laws? What kind of conversation proceeds from your heart on a Sunday afternoon regarding your pastor and elders at church? What do they hear after the policeman just wrote you a ticket?

Are we living with sensitivity within the broad range of relationships into which God has placed us? Are we showing others that we are under authority—God's authority—and it is our privilege to be there?

We mistakenly believe that we give respect to those in positions of authority because they have earned it. But respect cannot be based solely on personal or professional qualifications. Respect is based on the position that *God* has given that person. That position comes from God and demands our highest respect. Think of David in 1 Samuel 26 where we see him sparing Saul's life—and not for the first time. David knew that he had been appointed by God to be the next king over Israel. David also knew that Saul was out to murder him. Yet when David had the perfect opportunity and strong encouragement to kill Saul, what was his response? "The LORD forbid that I should put out my hand against the LORD's anointed" (1 Samuel 26:11). David submitted, even at the risk of losing his life, to the authority God had placed over him.

Let me apply this directly to us and to the honor due our parents, even after we have left our homes and established a new family. Your family has been established by God; you were placed into your family by him. Families were established by God to be those nearest and dearest to us. When God led his people out of Egypt and wanted to teach them how to live in freedom after four hundred years of slavery, he told them to honor their parents.

I find it amazing that this commandment is placed even before marital faithfulness. Of course, what child can respect his spouse if he never learned to respect his mother and father?

Let me ask you, are you honoring your parents? That word *honor* means to give them weight. Are they important to you? How are you showing it? Do they know they are important to you? Do they feel their importance in your schedule, in your budget, and in your conversations? Remember that this commandment does not say, "Honor your mother and father when they are good to you." All families struggle, but ignoring your family is not an option for a Christian.

Do you really know your parents? When was the last time you prayed for them, or with them? Do you know what their day looks like? Do you know who their closest contacts are outside the family? Do you know if they have needs?

You may be saying, "Wait a minute, Jani. You don't know *my* parents. They didn't meet my needs when I was small. They don't deserve my honor now." But this command is not optional for just those who have good parents. It does not say, "Honor your father and your mother when they are honorable." Nor does it say, "Honor your father and your mother until you have formed your own household."

Think of Jesus—he created his parents! In Luke 2:41–52, Jesus was twelve years old when he went with his family to Jerusalem to celebrate the Feast of the Passover. Afterward he chose to stay behind at the temple in Jerusalem when his parents set out on the return journey. His parents didn't understand him at all and were greatly distressed by his actions. Yet he returned with them and "was submissive to them" (v. 51).

We don't honor our parents because they deserve it. In fact, some of you may have had parents who were even abusive. We honor them because the nature of the gospel is that *God gives us what we don't deserve*. We don't do it for their sake—we do it for Jesus' sake. In other words, we don't honor our parents because they deserve it. We don't even honor them because we love God. We honor them because God loves us, and he gave them to us because he loves us, and he calls us to honor them because he loves us.

This commandment does not teach us how to have great families. It teaches us how to be great family members. So what are some ways we can honor our parents?

We can honor our parents by speaking kindly to and about them. Do you save your most glowing compliments for your best friend while speaking disparagingly of your parents? Are your conversations with your mother and father gracious and uplifting? "Let no corrupting talk come out of your mouths, but only such as is good for building up, as fits the occasion, that it may give grace to those who hear" (Ephesians 4:29).

We can honor our parents by showing them consideration. We can make time for them. Do you feel your duty is done with the Sunday afternoon phone call? Do you resent reaching out to them, including them, honoring them? "Love is patient and kind . . . it is not irritable or resentful" (1 Corinthians 13:4–5).

We can let them into our life and let them share our highs and lows. Do you share your deepest intimacies with the ladies in your Bible study but never open up to your parents? "Let your father and mother be glad; let her who bore you rejoice" (Proverbs 23:25). We can also provide for them. "If anyone does not provide for his relatives, and especially for members of his household, he has denied the faith and is worse than an unbeliever" (1 Timothy 5:8).

Do you take flowers to a shut-in at church but never go visit your parents? Are you happy to give money at the office for United Way or some other charity but never think to help your parents? Jesus warned us not to use our charitable giving as an excuse to forget our parents, in Matthew 15:4–6:

> "For God commanded, 'Honor your father and your mother,' and, 'Whoever reviles father or mother must surely die.' But you say, 'If anyone tells his father or his mother, "What you would have gained from me is given to God," he need not honor his father.' So for the sake of your tradition you have made void the word of God."

Do your parents feel honored by you? What are you doing to show them how important they are to God? Do your actions show them how much you sense God's love? What kind of family member are you?

Giving the Fifth Commandment

Not only must we model the fifth commandment; we must also require it of our children. We must help them understand how respect for authority is the thread that governs our society and ultimately preserves our freedom. They need to see that this is *from God*. In fact, God takes this so seriously that those who disobeyed were to be stoned to death, because their very freedom was at stake (Deuteronomy 21:18–21).

> Sometimes we feel that it is impossible to turn the tide of disrespectful youth.

> "One man complained, 'Youth today love luxury. They have bad manners, contempt for authority, no respect for older people, and talk nonsense when they should work. Young people do not stand up any longer when adults enter the room. They contradict their parents, talk too much in company, guzzle their food, lay their legs on the table, and tyrannize their elders.' Who was this man? It was Socrates, the philosopher who lived four hundred years before Christ! His words describe what young people are still like today because they describe what young people are always like."[1]

Children are our investment in the future. We must teach them a lifestyle of respect, not only by obeying this commandment ourselves, but also by requiring them to obey it. Why is this so hard? It's hard because requiring a child to obey takes a lot of energy, both physical and mental. Requiring respect is hard work!

Children disobey for two reasons: Either we let them, or the pain they have experienced from disobedience in the past is not enough of a deterrent to keep them from disobeying again. Children must learn that respect is not a matter of preference; it is a mandate from their eternal Father. And God has called you to teach that to your child. If you let your child disobey you, you are disobeying your heavenly Father. Honoring one's parents in the early years is largely manifested through obedience:

> Children, obey your parents in the Lord, for this is right. "Honor your father and mother" (this is the first commandment with a promise), "that it may go well with you and that you may live long in the land." (Ephesians 6:1–3)

Notice the phrase "in the Lord" in Ephesians 6:1. Children are not told to obey their parents in things morally wrong or against scriptural teaching. They are to obey their parents in those things consistent with Christ and his Word.

Why are children to obey their parents? They are to obey because parents stand in the place of God to their children, performing God-like functions (loving, providing, caring, protecting) as God's special agents. This is God's plan for passing down the faith through families to each new generation. When young children disobey their parents, they are rebelling against God. Disobedience to parents indicates a corrupt, out-of-control, anti-God spirit (2 Timothy 3:1–5).

Children are to obey because with few exceptions no one cares more for a child than a parent. They are also to obey because obedience pleases the Lord (Colossians 3:20). Additionally, obedience is required because that is the example Jesus set for us to follow (Luke 2:51). An obvious reason children are to obey is simply that it is the right thing to do (Ephesians 6:1). Finally, they must obey because doing so is in their best interest (Deuteronomy 5:16; Ephesians 6:3).

How can you best help your child to honor you? You can make obedience a part of your life. It must be just as much "be what I am" as it is "do what I say." Obedience is for all of God's children. You are under authority too—God's authority. And it is your privilege to be there. You can also define your priorities. What are you willing to go to the mat for? What's really important to you? Spend your energies there.

You can also follow through on your instructions until you have been obeyed. Say yes whenever you can. But when you say no, mean it. When your child hears a firm "No!" and survives the frustration that inevitably follows, he is strengthened. He has learned self-control and endurance, and will be better able to tell himself "no" when he is on his own.

Additionally, you can teach your child to respect people and property. In both words and actions kids must demonstrate that people and things are not targets for their scorn and wrath. Another way you can help your child to honor you is by making the pain of the discipline outweigh the pleasure of disobedience; without this, the discipline may be meaningless to your child. Finally, give many rewards. Children should learn that good and pleasure go together as surely as sin and pain. Reward cheerful obedience, good manners, kindness, respect, hard work—all those qualities that you long to see developed in your child.

The fifth commandment ends with a promise: ". . . that your days may be long in the land." This does not simply mean that anyone who obeys this command will live to old age. This is a Hebrew phrase for the fullness of God's blessing, an abundant life. Proverbs 3:1–2 says, "My son, do not forget my teaching, but let your heart keep my commandments, for length of days and years of life and peace they will add to you."

God is lovingly at work in this commandment enriching relationships. He is sensitizing every one of us to the privilege of belonging to one another. When his grace is upon us we discover who we are and how we fit in. And we discover how valuable other people are.

God's loving intentions are shown here in that this commandment is to *everyone's* advantage. Honoring our parents is for the sake of the kids. Do you want to live in a land where there is order and peace and courtesy and calm? Then see to it that you honor your parents and that the children in your life honor you. This will bring domestic and ecclesiastical and even national blessings.

STUDY AND DISCUSSION FOR LIVING THE FIFTH COMMANDMENT

1. Review the four commandments you have already memorized, and then add this one to memory. Review Psalm 119:18 and Deuteronomy 32:46–47. Write out all these verses two times this week as you seek to hide God's Word in your heart.

2. How does a parent-child relationship affect one's life, both inside and outside the home?

3. According to Scripture, who are the people God has placed in authority over you?

   - 1 Peter 2:13–17
   - Romans 13:1–7
   - 1 Peter 5:1–5
   - Hebrews 13:7, 17
   - Ephesians 5:22–24, 33

   Look over this list. Are there some who are not receiving your respect? Why? How can you better follow God's loving law here?

4. How can grown children obey the fifth commandment? Why is this so important? Read Proverbs 23:22, 1 Corinthians 13:4–6, and Ephesians 4:29. Are there some specific things God wants you to do to honor your parents?

5. Are you requiring the children in your life to respect you? Why or why not? What is the biblical basis for requiring children to honor the adults in their lives? Read Proverbs 3:1–2, Luke 2:51, and Ephesians 6:1–3.

STUDY AND DISCUSSION FOR GIVING THE FIFTH COMMANDMENT TO OUR CHILDREN

Materials needed: pen, Bible, tape, index card, and the big red heart.

1. Review the first four commandments with your child. See if you can say them to each other from memory. Discuss in what ways you (and your child, if appropriate) have broken them. Ask, "Is it possible for anyone to keep the laws God has given us?" (Romans 3:10–12). "Why would he give us laws that we can't keep? Do you think God is mad at us?"

2. Now is a perfect time to talk with your child about sin, God's holiness, and the perfect Law Keeper. Here are some verses to share: Romans 3:21–24; 7:21–8:8; 2 Corinthians 5:17–21. These are deep spiritual truths but can be grasped even by a young child. Ask God to help you show your child that no one has ever kept the law but Jesus. By dying for us, he took upon himself the punishment our disobedience deserves. When we look to Christ as our Savior, God looks at us through Christ's sacrifice and counts us as perfect as his precious Son.

3. Make a small cross out of the index card and tape it at the top of the mirror on your big red heart. Lift the cross and look into the mirror with your child, reviewing the way in which the law is like a mirror, showing us that we disobey God's commandments but are totally unable to cleanse us from our sin in any way. Now put the cross back over the mirror and tell your child, "Jesus came and kept these laws perfectly for you and me. He lived the life that God wants me to live. Then he died on the cross—the very death I deserve. Now when I honor and love Jesus, God looks at me through Jesus and gives me Jesus' perfect record." Ask your child if he would like to be reconciled to God, to be made right with him. If he does, ask him to pray with you and to tell God what is on his heart as he gives his life to God because of Christ's redeeming love.

4. Talk together about how the first four commandments show us ways to love God above all else, and how the next six tell us how to love each other. Read the fifth commandment and write it on your big red heart.

5. Discuss what *honor* means. Together look up *honor* and *respect* in the dictionary. Make sure your child understands that you, the parent, must obey this commandment as well. Read Romans 13:1; Ephesians 5:22-24; Hebrews 13:17; 1 Peter 5:5. What is God telling us to do in these verses?

Discuss the answer in terms of authority figures such as teachers, police, statesmen, and church leaders.

6. Read together Luke 2:50–51 and Ephesians 6:1–3. Talk about the benefits of obedience and why you insist on respect in your home.

7. In light of this commandment, decide on one new focus of behavior that each of you will work on this week. As the parent, you might decide to obey the speed limit or make a special sacrifice for one of your parents. Your child might work on obeying the first time he is told or talking respectfully about the adults in his life. The possibilities are endless. Note these on an index card and tape it near the fifth commandment on the big red heart. Plan to check with each other periodically to see how it is going.

CHAPTER SIX

A FOUNTAIN OF LIFE

"You shall not murder."

EXODUS 20:13

Lawrence and Ruth and their four young children came all the way from Kenya so that Lawrence could study at Trinity Evangelical Divinity School in Deerfield, Illinois, where Ray was teaching in the Old Testament department. Ruth and I became good friends. I remember my surprise when Ruth told me how very frightened she had been to bring her young family to Chicago. She thought they would encounter gunfights and carnage, for sure, as they stepped off the plane with their little ones. That was the America she had heard about in Kenya.

For many people outside the United States we are known as the most violent nation on earth. Is it any wonder? Think of our newscasts. Think of our entertainment. It is estimated that by the time a child is eighteen, he will have witnessed over two hundred thousand acts of violence on television alone.[1]

Retired military psychologist Lt. Col. David Grossman is an expert in teaching people to overcome their natural reluctance to kill someone. He was shocked to realize that children who watch TV and play violent video games are subjected to the same methods—the conditioning and desensitization—that the army uses to train soldiers.[2] We—our families, our schools, and our neighborhoods—are surrounded by death. Indeed, we live in a culture of death. "It is the constant presence of death that spoils the understanding of life! It was not meant to be so."[3]

HIS LOVING LAW

The sixth commandment reveals a God who values life. From this four-word command flows a river of biblical themes. We are not to injure others or ourselves in any way. The sanctity of human life is at the root of the Christian ethic. In the very first chapter of God's Word to us we see that God is the sovereign author of life, who alone has the right and power to give life. "So God created man in his own image, in the image of God he created him; male and female he created them" (Genesis 1:27). All life comes from God (Psalm 22:9; 139:13–16).

From Noah's day onward, God has required a reckoning for the life of a man. "Whoever sheds the blood of man, by man shall his blood be shed, for God made man in his own image" (Genesis 9:6). There is an account to settle for the life of every human being.

We are image bearers of God. His image is stamped upon every human being. Every person is created in God's likeness (James 3:9) and thus, by virtue of being human, possesses a divinely assigned dignity that doesn't depend on personal character or abilities. When I look at another human being, I am looking at a little bit of God, and therefore that person is worthy of honor because of whom he represents. In this commandment God loves us by teaching us the value of human life—my life, your life—and by requiring us to protect all of life, including our own.

We serve a God who commands us never to harm another with our actions, thoughts, words, or indifference.

The Bible teaches there are many ways to break this commandment. The first way is with our hands, our *actions*. It is obvious that this command demands that we not take another's life. This includes homicide, abortion, and euthanasia. Every human being, including the sick, the young, the helpless and the disabled, is made in the image of God and is of inestimable value in God's sight.

Some of you reading may have killed your baby in your womb, and there are deep scars there. That was a sin, but it was not the unpardonable sin. You have broken this commandment, but Jesus is ready to walk you through the cleansing power of his forgiveness. Come to him. Open your heart up to him. Seek help from a trusted counselor or pastor to foster healing.

The Bible teaches the only time that killing is justifiable is in cases of public justice, lawful war, or necessary defense, in other words, the killing that is necessary for the preservation of life. Now some of you are thinking, "Good! I am safe here. I haven't killed anyone. This is one commandment I can really keep!" But when God's law prohibits the evil act, it prohibits the impulse as well. God understands that every evil act springs from an evil impulse within.

There are other ways of breaking this command without actually taking someone's life. You can murder someone with your *thoughts*. 1 John 3:15 says, "Everyone who hates his brother is a murderer." We also read:

> "You shall not hate your brother in your heart, but you shall reason frankly with your neighbor, lest you incur sin because of him. You shall not take vengeance or bear a grudge against the sons of your own people, but you shall love your neighbor as yourself: I am the LORD." (Leviticus 19:17–18)

> "You have heard that it was said to those of old, 'You shall not murder; and whoever murders will be liable to judgment.' But I say to you that everyone who is angry with his brother will be liable to judgment." (Matthew 5:21–22).

No one can escape the force of these words. It bears repeating: when God's law prohibits the evil act, it prohibits the impulse as well. The Heidelberg Catechism puts it this way: "Do not dishonor, hate, injure, kill by thoughts, words, or gestures, much less by deeds" (paraphrase).

We are all murderers. We have murdered others through anger and hate. For instance, we fight against abortion because of the evil of murder. And that is right. But how do we feel about the abortionist? You see, God hates the root of murder—not just the act, but the root of the act. Murder starts in the heart. We are all too familiar with the expression, "If looks could kill . . ."

The sixth commandment calls us to examine ourselves right down to the root of the problem. Can we face this? We are not nice people having a bad thought now and then. We are evil people proving what we truly are, unable to control the anger and hatred that springs so readily from within our hearts.

There is a kind of genteel violence that we dish out to each other that the laws of the state do not—and should not—confront, but which God's law searchingly confronts:

> Now the works of the flesh are evident: . . . enmity, strife, jealousy, fits of anger, rivalries, dissensions, divisions, envy . . . and things like these. I warn you, as I warned you before, that those who do such things will not inherit the kingdom of God. But the fruit of the Spirit is love, joy, peace, patience, kindness, goodness, faithfulness, gentleness, self-control; against such things there is no law. (Galatians 5:19–23)

> What causes quarrels and what causes fights among you? Is it not this—that your passions are at war within you? You desire and do not have, so you murder. (James 4:1–2)

Do Christians behave like that? Do you? We all do! Think of the last time someone cut you off in traffic! Why do you think we need machines to give us numbers for service at the corner deli?

Not only do we murder others with our actions and thoughts; we also murder with our *words*. Jesus said, "You have heard that it was said to those of old, 'You shall not murder; and whoever murders will be liable to judgment.' But I say to you that . . . whoever insults his brother will be liable to the council; and whoever says, 'You fool!' will be liable to the hell of fire" (Matthew 5:21–22).

How many times have you called someone a name, either in

your heart, or out of their range of hearing, or, for that matter, to their face? The anger that produces that outburst shows what murderers we all are.

> There are six things that the LORD hates, seven that are an abomination to him: haughty eyes, a lying tongue, and hands that shed innocent blood, a heart that devises wicked plans, feet that make haste to run to evil, a false witness who breathes out lies, and one who sows discord among brothers. (Proverbs 6:16–19)

The Bible plainly connects those who gossip and slander with those who hate God (Romans 1:29–30). Gossip and slander are not only rampant on the newsstand. How many churches have been troubled, even divided, by someone murdering another with her tongue?

God loves us in this commandment by telling us how to treat the names, or reputations, of others. One of our Puritan fathers put it this way: "It is a great cruelty to murder a man in his name . . . it is an irreparable injury. No physician can heal the wounds of the tongue."[4]

There is a story told of a young man who came to a monk upset with himself over how he had spread a bad report about another. The monk told the young man to take a bag of feathers and put one on the doorstep of all whom he thought had heard his words. When the young man had finished, he returned to the monk, asking him what he should do next. The monk told him to retrace his steps and retrieve all those feathers. The young man grew quite agitated, exclaiming that was impossible, for by now the feathers had blown all over town. "Exactly," said the monk, "and so with your words; they are impossible to retrieve."

Why do we gossip? The Bible links busybodies with gossip (1 Timothy 5:13). We love to be "in the know." Gossip feeds our natural curiosity. It also raises our status by lowering that of another. Somehow, in our twisted, evil hearts, we feel better about ourselves if we can make another look bad.

Why do we slander? We slander because we are angry. We feel misused, misunderstood. We want to justify ourselves, and the only way we can is by showing how wrong another is and how right we are. The words of slander can murder someone's reputation just as a sword can murder someone's body.

> There is one whose rash words are like sword thrusts, but the tongue of the wise brings healing. (Proverbs 12:18)

> You shall not go around as a slanderer among your people, and you shall not stand up against the life of your neighbor. I am the LORD. (Leviticus 19:16)

Morally, what's the difference between a ghetto drive-by shooting and a church where people commit character assassination through slander? A cell phone can be just as much a murder weapon as a gun. What God sees are nasty murderers versus nice murderers; that's all. We all bite, devour, and destroy one another (Galatians 5:15). Who has not broken the sixth commandment?

Actions, thoughts, and words can all be used as murder weapons. We also murder others through *negligence*. We can murder someone through sins of omission as well as by sins of commission. Think of the story of the Good Samaritan in Luke 10:29–37. There are really several criminals in this parable: the original thugs who beat and robbed this poor traveler and the two other men who passed by, leaving him for dead when they could have helped him. All it takes to break this command is to do nothing at all!

OUR LASTING LEGACY

Living the Sixth Commandment

How do we live out the positive aspect of this commandment? We must do everything in our power to see to the health and welfare of our families and neighbors, as well as do everything to live life well ourselves. We must be *life givers*.

LIVE LIFE WELL YOURSELF

There are many ways in which we rob ourselves of life. We allow ourselves to live under such stress and fatigue that it robs us of years of life. How can we be life givers, living life well ourselves? First, we can be patient, bearing with the hand of God. Ponder David's actions in 1 Samuel 24:12 when he spared Saul's life. To live in an attitude of trust is to protect our life. This includes refraining from anger. "Be still before the LORD and wait patiently for him; fret not yourself over the one who prospers in his way, over the man who carries out evil devices! Refrain from anger and forsake wrath! Fret not yourself; it tends only to evil" (Psalm 37:7–8).

Did you know that another way to be a life giver is to have a cheerful spirit? "A joyful heart is good medicine, but a crushed spirit dries up the bones" (Proverbs 17:22). In fact, this commandment even warns against immoderate grief, that is, grief that we allow to get out of control. "Worldly grief produces death" (2 Corinthians 7:10). Personal devastation over hurts and sorrows can be a form of self-murder.

A third way we can weaken our lives by disobeying this command is found in Proverbs 14:30: "A tranquil heart gives life to the flesh, but envy makes the bones rot." Envy corrodes us inside where no one can see. Envy is to the body what termites are to the foundation of a home.

A fourth way we can disobey this command is through neglecting our bodies through intemperance of any sort, such as excesses in diet. It has been said that many dig their graves with their mouths. Are you willing to obey this command by preserving your own life through healthy habits of diet and exercise? Self-hatred is really self-murder. And the Bible prohibits this in any form, from suicide to eating yourself into the grave.

Give Life to Others

God shows us that we obey this command by being *life giving* to others, rather than *life depleting*. There is no other way to be a Christian. Are you a life giver? What can you do and say that others may have life? Where can you bring more life? Who needs your heart, your time, your words, or your money?

What can we do to promote life, to cherish and honor and care and protect this gift we have received from God? Here are some suggestions. See what you can add to this list:

- Pray and work on the behalf of the unborn, the elderly, and the disabled. We must protect the innocent. We dare not stand by while others are injured; otherwise we participate in their harm. Proverbs 31:8–9 says, "Open your mouth for the mute, for the rights of all who are destitute. Open your mouth, judge righteously, defend the rights of the poor and needy." And the psalmist wrote, "Give justice to the weak and the fatherless; maintain the right of the afflicted and the destitute. Rescue the weak and the needy; deliver them from the hand of the wicked" (Psalm 82:3–4).
- Help the children whom you so long to see born rather than murdered in the womb. Our responsibility does not end in the labor room. Many children need foster care and adoption.
- Care for the sick and dying and give to the oppressed. Do you care for others? It is oftentimes so much easier to send money to the orphan on TV while neglecting the recent divorcee in our Sunday school class. Jesus identifies so completely with the needy that whatever is done for them, he considers done to himself (Matthew 25:34 ff.). When we see to the necessities of others we are obeying this command. The more good and helpful we are, the more like God we are. Psalm 119:68 says, "You are good and do good." There are many ways we can't be like God. But we *can* be merciful and kind to those near to us. Ask God to give you eyes to see the suffering around you. Open your heart to another's heartache. Give your time and love and kindness and mercy and energy. This is God's call to us in the sixth commandment.
- We must love our neighbor. Love is the opposite of hatred and murder. "Owe no one anything, except to love each other, for the one who loves another has fulfilled the law. For the commandments, 'You shall not commit adultery, You shall not murder, You shall not steal, You shall not covet,' and any other commandment, are summed up in this word: 'You shall love your neighbor as yourself.' Love does no wrong to a neighbor; therefore love is the fulfilling of the law" (Romans 13:8–10). Do you even know your neighbor?
- Let your words be a "fountain of life" (Proverbs 10:11). This is soul work. How can you help another toward heaven? What can you say

that will bring healing and life to another? Does someone you know need words of kindness, words of healing, words of forgiveness, words of life?

How can we ever be all that this short command requires? Who hasn't broken the sixth commandment in thought or word or deed? No one—no one but Jesus. He has gone before us, obeying this commandment perfectly. He was murdered, though he only gave life. He is the ultimate life-giver, and we are called to enjoy his forgiveness for our own murderous actions, thoughts, words, and negligence. As he transfers his love and grace onto us, we in turn can give his life to others.

Giving the Sixth Commandment

Raising a child within our culture of death is a great challenge. How can we help our children to become life-givers rather than life-drainers? We can teach our children how to resolve conflict without turning to violence. We can insist that they control their angry outbursts. Emotions are just as much a part of our sin nature as our minds and souls (Proverbs 29:11; James 4:2). We must monitor the amount of violence our children watch on TV and limit their exposure to violent video games. Desensitizing our youth to murder is robbing them of life.

We must teach our children what it means to be made in the image of God. Let them see in our homes and beyond how much we value life. We can talk about what it means to be a life-giver. Who, in our sphere of influence, needs more life-giving love? Let's help our children to see that we all need Jesus, the perfect life-giver, to fill us with himself, so we can begin to look beyond our own desires and needs.

What a miracle of grace that angry, hateful, slanderers like us are becoming life-givers! God is making us into people whose very character fulfills the sixth commandment. He is circumcising our hearts, putting his words into our mouths and hearts, and making us into people who not only would not hurt each other, but who positively enrich and energize each other. This is the gospel of Jesus Christ.

STUDY AND DISCUSSION FOR LIVING THE SIXTH COMMANDMENT

1. Review the first five commandments and learn the sixth. Review Psalm 119:18 and Deuteronomy 32:46–47. Say them out loud two times this week to a family member or friend.

2. Read Genesis 1:27; 9:6; Psalm 139:13–16; and James 3:9. What does it mean to be made in the image of God? How does bearing his image make abortion, euthanasia, suicide, and homicide wrong?

3. What are some ways we can break this command without actually taking someone's life? Use these verses to help you answer:

   - 1 John 3:15
   - Leviticus 19:16–18
   - Matthew 5:21–22
   - James 4:1–2
   - Proverbs 12:18

4. Read Luke 10:29–37. How did the robbers, the priest, and the Levite all break the sixth commandment? How did the Samaritan keep it?

5. What is our obligation to take care of our own lives? Conversely, how do we rob ourselves of life? Read Psalm 37:7–8; Proverbs 17:22; Proverbs 14:30; and Philippians 3:19.

6. Where is God calling you to be a life-giver? (Matthew 25:34–46; Romans 13:8–10). Whose soul needs more life poured into it through love and kindness and generosity? How can you help another toward heaven by fulfilling this commandment?

STUDY AND DISCUSSION FOR GIVING THE SIXTH COMMANDMENT TO OUR CHILDREN

Materials needed: Bible, marker, photograph of your family or child, tape, calendar, the big red heart.

1. Read together Exodus 20:13. Copy this commandment onto your big red heart.

2. Read Genesis 9:6 and Psalm 139:13–16 with your child, and discuss what it means to be made in God's image. Look at a photo of your family or your child. Talk about how it would feel to see someone draw ugly marks on the photo or tear it up, and, therefore, how much more precious is a life! Tape the picture onto the big red heart next to the sixth commandment. Next to it write, "We bear God's image in us."

3. Talk about hatred with your child. Do you allow the word *hate* to be used in your home? Why or why not?

4. Show your child how this commandment can be broken without ever touching another person's body.

    - 1 John 3:15
    - Proverbs 12:18
    - Matthew 5:21–22

5. Read Luke 10:29–37 together. Talk about how we can disobey this commandment by indifference or neglect. We are to be life-givers. Discuss with your child how we should define the word *neighbor* from this parable.

6. Read Romans 13:8 with your child. Talk about someone your family knows who needs more life-giving love. Decide how you can bring life to this person. Together write out a concrete plan on your calendar.

CHAPTER SEVEN

MARRIAGE: MAYHEM OR MELODY?

"You shall not commit adultery."

EXODUS 20:14

HIS LOVING LAW

Every marriage should be a love story. No one enters marriage thinking, "How can I ruin this? How can I bring pain and despair and ugliness and misery to all the people closest to me?" And yet over half of our marriages end in divorce. Do you know anyone who has not been touched through family or friends by the devastation of marital chaos?

How loving God is to us in this command! He shows us the way to romantic, happy marriages and solid, secure families. "Walk as children of light (for the fruit of light is found in all that is good and right and true), and try to discern what is pleasing to the Lord" (Ephesians 5:8–10). "For this is the will of God, your sanctification: that you abstain from sexual immorality; that each one of you know how to control his own body in holiness and honor" (1 Thessalonians 4:3–4).

The Magnificence of Marriage

God's Word is unashamedly pro-romance. Think of all the love stories in it: Abraham and Sarah, Isaac and Rebekah, Jacob and

Rachel, Ruth and Boaz, and others. Think of the passages that are erotic, like the Song of Solomon and Proverbs 5:15–19. God celebrates love and sex in marriage. God values our sexuality and calls for us to enjoy this beautiful gift within the security of marital commitment. This is where faithful devotion and lasting love can best promote the joy of a one-flesh relationship.

Think of the blessings of marriage. You belong somewhere and with someone. Someone has chosen you, and you have had the chance to choose someone for yourself. You enter into a relationship of trust and comfort and joy. You write your own shared history. Marriage makes two people what they could never be alone. God, in his great mercy and love for us, has given us the seventh commandment to protect the joy, love, pleasure, and security that only marriage can offer.

From the beginning, God has placed a high value on our sexuality. He made us male and female as part of his "very good" creation (Genesis 1:27, 31). God led Eve to the man to be his partner in the challenge of life (Genesis 2:18–24). Jesus, a single man, honored marriage when he said, "What therefore God has joined together, let not man separate" (Matthew 19:6). He honored a wedding with his presence and his first miracle (John 2).

The Bible teaches that marriage is to be sacred, hallowed, and inviolable. It is to be a bond between a man and a woman for the duration of their life on earth. The Bible also teaches that everyone is to honor marriage. "Let marriage be held in honor among all, and let the marriage bed be undefiled, for God will judge the sexually immoral and adulterous" (Hebrews 13:4).

The Devastation of Adultery

This commandment prohibits any and all sexual activity outside of marriage. It is for our protection and the protection of those around us, including our children. Why is adultery so bad? It is bad because it takes a unique and rare treasure—the very mystery of two human beings building a one-flesh relationship—and smashes this mystical union with the hammer of reckless selfishness.

Adultery brings misery into so many relationships. It harms the adulterer with disgust, disease, and self-hatred. It introduces a nagging betrayal into the marriage. It shows our children that our personal pleasure is more important than honor, and that our satisfaction is more important than their security. It undercuts the two best joys that thrive in a family—love and peace.

The seventh commandment not only forbids adultery; it also forbids everything that leads up to adultery. God is confronting *all* sexual sin, right down to our inmost thoughts. In Matthew 5:27–30 Jesus teaches us that this command confronts all sexual sin. Jesus is not talking about sexual curiosity. Nor is he talking about an invasive sexual thought that someone resists and about which someone cries out to God for help. What Jesus is talking about is fantasizing—sustaining and cultivating a little sexual experience in your imagination and then guarding this mental habit from repentance.

This commandment forbids our looking at another and imagining the sexual possibilities. It forbids lusting after the attention of a man who is not my husband. It forbids flirting. It forbids cultivating my primary emotional support structure with a man who is not my husband.

Somehow we have a higher tolerance for our inward sins than for our outward sins. But we must not caress a secret world of lust and fantasy, prizing it more than the spiritual pleasures we have in Christ.

God is very clear about this area of our lives. He takes sexual sins very seriously. Shouldn't we? Adultery without repentance damns the soul (1 Corinthians 6:9–10). Do you realize what God is saying? Cultivating a life of sexual sin means we are prizing our secret world of pleasure more than Christ. He says that those who evidence "sexual immorality, impurity, sensuality . . . will not inherit the kingdom of God" (Galatians 5:19–21). Adultery is a mature sin. It is a deliberate sin. You may *fall* in love, but you *walk* yourself into that stranger's bedroom.

How can we guard against adultery in all its various forms? We can learn to keep our promises day by day in the small things. Then it will be harder for us to break the most sacred oath we have ever taken—our marriage vow. We can avoid difficult or tempting situations. Are we asking God to keep us from getting burned while we continue to run our finger through the candle flame? Our bodies are the very temple of the Holy Spirit whom God has given us at great cost to himself (1 Corinthians 6:18–20).

Be diligent with your heart. Proverbs 4:23 says, "Keep your heart with all vigilance, for from it flow the springs of life." Guard our hearts. What kind of people do you admire and long to be with and to be like? "Do not be deceived: 'Bad company ruins good morals'" (1 Corinthians 15:33). Sin is a very catching disease. Also guard your eyes and your time (remember David and Bathsheba in 2 Samuel 11:4). "Turn my eyes from looking at worthless things; and give me life in your ways" (Psalm 119:37).

But the best guard against adultery is a deep love and satisfaction in Jesus Christ alone. This is true for both married and single people. The soul that is drinking deeply from his fountain of life is not going to crave drinks from lesser joys. What is it about Christ that is unsatisfying to you? His lovingkindness is not only better than sex; it is better than life itself! (Psalm 63:3)

The question for each one of us *should never be*, "How far can I go with a relationship, either in fantasy or reality, before it becomes a sin?" The question *should always be*, "How can I go so deep with Jesus Christ that sexual purity is the glad outworking of my joyful satisfaction in him?"

Ultimately, adultery, like all sin, is a heart issue. This is where it begins. And the only one in the universe who can satisfy the desires of my heart is God, through his Son, Jesus Christ. Even the best of men (and I am married to one of them) will fail us, as we will fail them. The reason people seek after sinful pleasure is that they have not experienced real pleasure in Christ.

OUR LASTING LEGACY

Living the Seventh Commandment

God says that he hates divorce (Malachi 2:16). Why? He hates divorce because marriage is uniquely a symbol of Christ and the church in love (Ephesians 5:22–31). Every divorce represents division, discord, anger, and sin. Some of you reading this have gone through the horrors of a divorce. You know firsthand the pain and disgust and tragic repercussions that ensue from this severance of a one-flesh relationship torn apart.

And all of us have played with adultery, in our mind if not with our body. Infidelity can mean more than adultery. It can be unfaithfulness to our vow to love, cherish, honor, and obey our husbands. *No one* has kept this commandment perfectly—no one but our Savior, who kept it in our place. While adultery is a terrible sin, it is not the unpardonable sin. No one can sin herself outside the love of God because of adultery. But we must hear and heed Christ's words in John 8:11, "Neither do I condemn you; go, and from now on sin no more."

What legacy can we leave for the coming generations? Each commandment is two-sided. While prohibiting something, it also promotes the opposite. This commandment is promoting the beauty of a holy and honored romance between one man and one woman in the bond of sacred marriage.

How can we promote strong marriages in the years ahead? First of all, we can guard our spirit, as we are told in Malachi 2:13–15. Someone once said, "Marriages are made in heaven. But so are lightning and thunder." How are you guarding your spirit against the storms of life?

We are all like the proverbial puddle. We look clear enough until someone steps in and stirs up what's inside to cloud that once-clear water. What rises to your surface when you are agitated? Are you disappointed in your husband, his earning power, his lack of personal drive, his time-consuming hobbies? Are you frustrated by his spiritual malaise, conflicts with the in-laws, your less-than-thrilling times of intimacy, his inability to understand your moods and needs? Is there simmering beneath your exterior a longing to be free from the inevitable confinements of a lifetime promise? Marriage has to be an unconditional commitment to an imperfect person. That commitment means *a willingness to be unhappy sometimes*!

Guard your spirit, "For out of the heart come evil thoughts . . . adultery, sexual immorality . . ." (Matthew 15:19). Feed your soul with the things of God, not the sewage of this earth. One way to guard your spirit is to have a daily encounter with the Lover of your soul, Jesus Christ. Are you spending time in the Scriptures, letting the word of Christ dwell in you richly? Think of how much time you spent yesterday listening to the radio, watching the news or other TV programs or videos, reading the newspaper, occupying your mind with language and scenes that tempt you to unhappiness and unholiness.

When Jesus speaks of sexual sins in Matthew 5:27–30, he uses strong language: tear out your eye, cut off your hand. In other words, *be willing to endure pain to leave sinful habits behind*. Guard your spirit.

Secondly, set your heart and body toward your husband. You must love your mate with all you have. It is not just having a husband, but loving him, that makes you live in unity with him. You see, you really marry three people: the one you thought you knew, the one he really is, and the one he will become by being married to you. What will your husband become by being married to you? Will he be helped to obey this command by your loving, willing, happy response to him? Happily married women know that having a husband does not make a marriage anymore than having a piano makes a musician!

Study your mate. Do you understand his needs? Your husband needs admiration and respect. He needs you to appreciate and value him. Are you proud of him? (See Ephesians 5:33.)

Never think she loves him wholly
Never believe her love is blind

All his faults are locked securely
In a closet of her mind.[1]

He needs a home to retreat to for quiet and peace and refuge. Have you created that for him? (See Proverbs 9:13; 19:13; 21:9, 19; 25:24.)

Your husband needs a woman of inner and outer beauty. He needs to be proud of you in public and also in private. Does your husband find you attractive and tasteful? (See Song of Solomon 1:8–10; 2:2; 6:10; 1 Peter 3:1–5.)

Your husband needs sexual fulfillment. The Bible talks much about sexual intimacy. God delights in the romance of marital love. If your husband obeys this commandment, you will be the only God-blessed source of sexual enjoyment that he will ever experience. Give him the joy and pleasure that one can only experience within the security of a godly marriage. Proverbs 5 tells your husband to be intoxicated with your love. Are you helping him obey the Lord in this loving command? If your sex life doesn't become all it can be, your marriage can still survive. Sex isn't everything, but your marriage will have a soft spot, a vulnerable side where Satan can attack. (See Proverbs 5:14–20; Song of Solomon 4:9–5:1; and 1 Corinthians 7:1–5.)

I once heard a beautiful love story of a family celebrating their parents' fiftieth wedding anniversary:

> Last weekend my parents left on a long-awaited trip to Hawaii. They were as excited as if it were their honeymoon. When my parents married, they had only enough money for a three-day trip fifty miles from home. They made a pact that each time they made love, they would put a dollar in a special metal box and save it for a honeymoon in Hawaii for their fiftieth anniversary. Dad was a policeman, and Mom was a schoolteacher. They lived in a modest house and did all their own repairs. Raising five children was a challenge, and sometimes money was short. But no matter what emergency came up, Dad would not let Mom take any money out of the "Hawaii account." As the account grew, they put it in a savings account and then bought CDs.

My parents were always very much in love. I can remember Dad's coming home and telling Mom, "I have a dollar in my pocket," and she would smile at him and reply, "I know how to spend it." When each of us children married, Mom and Dad gave us a small metal box and told us their secret, which we found enchanting. All five of us are now saving for our dream honeymoons.

Mom and Dad never told us how much money they had managed to save, but it must have been considerable because when they cashed in those CDs, they had enough for airfare to Hawaii plus hotel accommodations for ten days and plenty of spending money. As they told us good-bye before leaving, Dad winked and said, "Tonight we are starting an account for Cancun. That should only take twenty-five years!"

Giving the Seventh Commandment

We must teach this commandment well to our children. Somehow we can teach them about stealing and lying and envy, but when it comes to sexual purity we are tongue-tied. Our children must *see and hear* from a very early age what God's loving plan is for them, because his way is so foreign to our culture. As Edith Schaeffer says, "What can unclean mean when a person lives in mud and filth?"

Do you model sexual purity for your children? Here's how one mother demonstrated sexual sensitivity. My friend Julie was starring as Maria in her local production of *The Sound of Music*. She faced a decision when her director instructed her to kiss the captain in one of the scenes where they are falling in love. Julie and her husband, John, are striving to raise their six children to love God and follow his ways. Their children have been taught that Mommy and Daddy love each other and never flirt with other people. Julie knew that her children would come to the play and have many questions about her kissing another man, whether it was acting or not! So she talked with the director, explaining her dilemma. They finally decided on the captain kissing her hand—a compromise accepted all around.

Our children must understand that sex joins a man and a woman in a profound way. That's why sex belongs only in marriage. The Bible's view is "leave and cleave" (see Genesis 2:24). The world's view is "cleave and leave." The world trivializes sex, but the Bible beautifies it. God, our creator, is the only one qualified to define for us the true profundity of sex.

As children develop an awareness of the sexual union blessed by God in marriage, they must hear that sex is more than a physical tension that two people release when they have intercourse. Sexual intimacy is a precious gift that is to be treated with tenderness and awe. Through it you expose not only your body, but your very soul, and overexposure will damage you in ways that are not always discernible at the moment of passion. Have you ever tried to separate two pieces of paper that are glued together? You have to rip and tear and destroy both pieces to separate them. Wrong things get stuck together when you have sex outside of marriage, and trying to get them unstuck rips apart your soul.

Train your children in the value of waiting. Help them to see that their virginity is a priceless treasure they will someday give to their spouse. Tell them that the love and attention an extra-marital relationship brings is too high a price to pay for their purity. Teach them to treasure their sexuality as much as God does.

As your child learns to trust God in other things, he will be able to trust God here. God made romance and he knows best how it works. I have never counseled a woman who said, "I wish we hadn't waited until we were married to have sex—I really missed out!" But I have wept with many who have been deeply hurt over the loss of their purity before marriage.

Our children need to develop a sense of honor that surpasses impulse. Let's begin training them at a young age. Help them learn a lifelong pattern of sacrifice, self-denial, and purity, of putting others before self, and God above all. If others ridicule them, pity the mockers, and remind your child that on his honeymoon he will have the last laugh.

God is calling our children to himself. And God, not sex, is the ultimate human experience. God honors those who honor him. Does your child see this lived out in your life?

If you have sinned in this area, or if your child has, then you know the shame and regret that follow. I want to tell you that there is a God in heaven who makes all things new. He is your Creator, and he can become your Re-Creator. Through Christ, God is reconciling all sorts of sinners to himself, letting the old pass away and making us a new creation (2 Corinthians 5:17–21). You don't have to keep looking at your past. You can look to your future and see God in his mercy opening up a new tomorrow for you.

The way into that new tomorrow is through repentance and faith. In repentance you turn away from all sin and turn toward God. What does this turning away look like? Well, where are you being tempted? Maybe you need to give up your favorite TV show, where you keep imagining that you are the one in that handsome actor's arms. Perhaps it is your reading material that's sending you into someone else's bed. Or you may even need to change your job if a relationship there, either in fantasy or reality, is leading you into any form of adultery.

And then as you turn away from your sin, turn toward God. Seek him in the Scriptures and through prayer. In faith, take that sin you have committed and push it over toward Christ. He is the only one who has ever kept this commandment perfectly. Let him carry your burden away. Let him bear it on the cross for you. He will give you, or your child, a bright new hope for the future. He is the one who said, "Neither do I condemn you; go, and from now on sin no more" (John 8:11).

STUDY AND DISCUSSION FOR LIVING THE SEVENTH COMMANDMENT

1. Review the first six commandments and learn the seventh. Write out all of them.

2. Review your memory verses from Psalm 119:18 and Deuteronomy 32:46–47. Recite them to a family member or friend. Have the listener sign here afterward for accountability. ____________________

3. Study Ephesians 5:8–10 and 1 Thessalonians 4:3–8. In the area of marital love, what pleases the Lord? What makes adultery so offensive to him?

4. Using the Scriptures in 3. above, as well as Matthew 5:27–30 and Colossians 3:5–6, begin an inventory of what this commandment prohibits.

5. How can you guard your heart against the temptations of adultery in all its various forms? Use these verses (and others you can think of) to note God's counsel to us:

   - Proverbs 4:23
   - 1 Corinthians 15:33
   - 2 Samuel 11:1–2
   - Psalm 119:11
   - Psalm 119:37
   - Psalm 119:24
   - Psalm 37:4

6. Based on the passages below, what are some ways you can promote strong marriages?

   - Malachi 2:13–16
   - Ephesians 5:33
   - Proverbs 19:13; 21:9
   - 1 Peter 3:1–6
   - Proverbs 5:15–20

7. Can you defend this statement: "God's Word is unashamedly pro-romance"? What is God's purpose in giving us the seventh commandment? How can you help the young people around you to honor marriage?

8. Spend some time praying for the marriages that your life touches.

STUDY AND DISCUSSION FOR GIVING THE SEVENTH COMMANDMENT TO OUR CHILDREN

Materials needed: Bible, marker, paper, glue, a bucket of water with dirt settled on the bottom (unless you can go outside and find a puddle!), a pitcher of clear water, and the big red heart.

Please note that this is an age-sensitive topic, and adjust these ideas as appropriate for your child. However, be sure to explain adultery as fully as your child can comprehend. Younger children can understand the wrongness of physical contact with someone other than a marriage partner. Older children can begin to understand the great mystery and sanctity of marital love.

1. Review the first six commandments with your child. Read Exodus 20:14 and write it on your big red heart.

2. Glue two pieces of paper together. While they are drying, read and discuss Matthew 19:4–6. Talk with your child about how love unites two people in a very special way, and that this union is good because it is from God. Include the truth that wrong things get stuck together when you love and kiss (or have sex with) someone you are not married to. Explain the way in which love glues people to one another, so if they separate, each takes a part of the other with him, causing both to end up torn and hurting. Try to pull the pieces of paper apart.

3. Read Malachi 2:15 and Proverbs 4:23. Discuss what it means to guard one's spirit. Use these verses to help your child hear God's counsel to her:

   - Psalm 119:11
   - Psalm 119:37
   - 1 Corinthians 15:33

4. Use the bucket or puddle to talk about the true condition of the human heart. Demonstrate how things can be hidden in our hearts until a temptation comes along and stirs things up. Stir the water and see how it gets all murky. Show your child what will happen if you leave the water. What happens to the dirt—does it go away? Pour out the dirty water, using it as a symbol for turning away from temptations and sin.

5. Rinse out the bucket and pour in fresh water while reading John 4:13–14 to your child. Help him begin to develop an understanding of his soul needs. Each human being has inner longings, soul thirsts, which only God can truly satisfy. Read Psalm 36:7–9 and talk about God's "river of delights."

6. Older children must hear from us that sexual union is more than mere physical pleasure, wonderful as that is! Marital love is a gift from God to be treated with tenderness and awe (Hebrews 13:4). Tell your child about the rewards of waiting and the painful disasters of playing around. Surround your child with as many healthy marriages as you can. And pray for the purity of your child and that of his future life partner.

CHAPTER EIGHT

LIVING ON EARTH AS CITIZENS OF HEAVEN

"You shall not steal."

EXODUS 20:15

HIS LOVING LAW

Tricia Lewis was my best friend in the earliest years of my childhood. She lived next door and was a whole year older than me. We played together constantly, and when she told me our stuffed animals and dolls got up and played together at night while we slept, I believed her. After all, when you are five and just starting kindergarten, first-graders seem so very smart.

We had many happy hours of playing together. But one day I ruined it. If you grew up in the fifties, you know how very important Pop Beads were to a little girl. Pop Beads were those little plastic, pastel beads that we used for necklaces and bracelets. Tricia had her own Pop Beads, and I had none. Oh, how I wanted some!

You know what happened, don't you? (Tricia, if you are reading this, please forgive me. I never fessed up to you!) Yes, one day when I was alone in Tricia's room, I stole some. Five years old and already a thief! And the problem was I couldn't even wear them! Tricia might see them, and my mother would surely be suspicious!

A Culture of Theft

Do you have a childhood memory of stealing? A cookie? A quarter? A toy? A test answer? If only stealing were confined to childhood! Unfortunately, we live in a culture that is dead to the shame of thievery. We live our daily lives in the psychological conditions that make stealing unshocking. Think of all our cultural theft:

- Tax theft. We falsify our tax returns, thinking our taxes are too high anyway. Some prominent voices have said that if everyone paid what they truly owe in taxes the national debt would disappear.
- Customs theft. We choose not to disclose various purchases.
- Credit card theft. We buy on credit what we have no intention or even ability to pay back.
- Borrowing theft. We don't return things people have loaned us.
- Welfare theft. We live off the government unnecessarily.
- Computer theft. We pilfer copyrighted software and CDs.
- Employee theft. This kind of thievery is so rampant, we hardly notice it anymore. We steal our employers' time and property. When we fail to put in a full day's work or call in sick when we just want a day off, we are stealing. We use business phones for personal business. We use office time for personal e-mails, surfing the Internet, or playing Solitaire, which is robbing our employers of our productivity. We steal office supplies, from paper clips to staplers. Philip Ryken writes, "This affects all of us. According to some estimates, as much as one-third of a product's cost goes to cover the various forms of stealing that occur on its way to the marketplace. This 'theft surcharge,' as analysts call it, is a drag on our whole economy."[1]
- Management theft. We demand longer hours and more work than the contract allows, or we pay inadequate wages.
- Plagiarism. We use someone else's ideas without attribution, which robs someone of his creativity and hard work.
- Time theft. We steal someone's time when we are late for an appointment.
- Reputational theft. We gossip and slander, stealing someone's good name.

Good name in man and woman, dear my lord,
Is the immediate jewel of their souls.
Who steals my purse, steals trash;
'tis something, nothing;
'Twas mine, 'tis his and has been slave to thousands;
But he that filches from me my good name
Robs me of that which not enriches him
And makes me poor indeed.[2]

- Giving theft. We withhold our tithes. But God says, "Will a man rob God? Yet you rob me in tithes and offerings" (Malachi 3:8).[3]

Watch Out for Number One!

Truly we have all sinned and fall short of the glory of God. In fact, we are so fallen, we hardly recognize our sinfulness. We feel sorry for ourselves and tell ourselves how unfair life is. Our souls grow accustomed to thoughts that make stealing plausible. *We live with an ownership mentality* that doesn't recognize the roots of stealing deep down in our souls so that robbing God and others somehow feels justified.

We tend to dwell in psychological conditions that make stealing justifiable because we don't really believe that God is watching out for us. Stealing says, "I know best what is fair and right. I am the master of my ways, and I had better watch out for myself." But God knows that stealing eats away at our souls. It deadens our sense of the love of God because we aren't waiting on God to provide. It destroys our self-respect because when we steal, we can't be proud of what we gain. Stealing leads to emptiness and isolation.

So God comes to us in the eighth commandment saying, "I have established certain boundaries in your life together. I love you and delight to provide for you. Live within the distribution system that I have ordained." God loves us in this commandment by coming to us in simplicity and telling us that stealing, in any of its various forms, is rebellion against the providence of God.

Loving Your Neighbor as Yourself

This commandment goes beyond prohibiting taking something that doesn't belong to us. It teaches us that we must respect and protect another's property as if it were our own. Scripture illuminates the eighth commandment in all realms of life.

First, *each one must bear his own weight.* "If anyone does not provide for his relatives, and especially for members of his household, he has denied the faith and is worse than an unbeliever" (1 Timothy 5:8); "Let the thief no longer steal, but rather let him labor, doing honest work with his own hands, so that he may have something to share with anyone in need" (Ephesians 4:28); "A slack hand causes poverty, but the hand of the diligent makes rich" (Proverbs 10:4). Paul "stayed with them and worked, for they were tentmakers by trade. And he reasoned in the synagogue every Sabbath, and tried to persuade Jews and Greeks" (Acts 18:3–4).

Second, *there are no "finders keepers, losers weepers" in the Bible.* "You shall not see your brother's ox or his sheep going astray and ignore them. You shall take them back to your brother . . . or with any lost thing of your brother's, which he loses and you find; you may not ignore it" (Deuteronomy 22:1–4). "If you meet your enemy's ox or his donkey going astray, you shall bring it back to him. If you see the donkey of one who hates you lying down under its burden, you shall refrain from leaving him with it; you shall rescue it with him" (Exodus 23:4–5). You may be thinking, as I am, I have to help even my *enemy*? But that is how God loves us. He is on a massive rescue operation to make his enemies his friends through the dying love of Jesus Christ.

Third, we must *give others what we owe them.* "Pay to all what is owed to them: taxes to whom taxes are owed, revenue to whom revenue is owed, respect to whom respect is owed, honor to whom honor is owed. Owe no one anything, except to love each other, for the one who loves another has fulfilled the law" (Romans 13:7–8). Do you realize that you can steal by not giving someone what you owe him? Taxes, revenue, respect, honor, even forgiveness—is it time for you to pay up?

Fourth, *give to others what they need.* "If anyone has the world's goods and sees his brother in need, yet closes his heart against him, how does God's love abide in him? Little children, let us not love in word or talk but in deed and in truth" (1 John 3:17–18).

Fifth, *refrain from greedy lawsuits.* "To have lawsuits at all with one another is already a defeat for you. Why not rather suffer wrong? Why not rather be defrauded? But you yourselves wrong and defraud—even your own brothers!" (1 Corinthians 6:7–8). We live in a culture of greed and self-promotion. "Whatever else may happen, I must get what is due me. It's my right! (At least that's what the commercials tell me.)" But think of the cost to society. If you have friends who are in medical practice, you know that the threat of lawsuit has forced some to quit their calling because they could not afford the rising costs of malpractice insurance.

Ray and I were faced with this kind of decision one spring. I had become very sick with a nasty infection that wasn't responding to normal antibiotics, so my doctor admitted me to the hospital. After three days of double doses of strong medicines, my fever was finally beginning to subside. I was hoping to go home in a day or two when a very busy nurse inadvertently gave me someone else's intravenous medication, which happened to be insulin. Over the next three hours I went into insulin shock and was quite sick again for a few days.

I was surprised when one of the nurses at our hospital, who also happened to be a friend from church, asked Ray and me to sue the hospital so management would see how overworked the staff was. I was even more surprised at my initial reaction! "Hmmm, let's see now, we could pay off our minivan, set up a college fund, take the kids to Disney World . . ." Many people insinuated we could go for broke. After some deep soul-searching, we decided this kind of lawsuit would not be money we could spend with a clear conscience. So we ended up agreeing that the hospital would cover my expenses and left it at that.

OUR LASTING LEGACY

Living the Eighth Commandment

God loves us in this command by showing us that we are to be givers, not takers. The kind of God who would say, "You shall not steal," is a generous, lavish, extravagant God. He is a God who "richly provides us with everything to enjoy" (1 Timothy 6:17). He is a God "who did not spare his own Son but gave him up for us all, [so] how will he not also with him graciously give us all things?" (Romans 8:32). He is the God who said, "It is done! I am the Alpha and the Omega, the beginning and the end. To the thirsty I will give from the spring of the water of life without payment" (Revelation 21:6).

Think what this world would be like with no locks on homes and cars and boats and bicycles. Think what it would be like if you lost your purse and didn't have to worry about canceling bank accounts and charge cards. What if we didn't have to worry about identity theft or cheating at school or IRS audits or security gates? You know what that would be? That would be heaven on earth. It would be a world of love. And that is how God is calling us to live—as citizens of heaven even while we remain here on earth. Part of his redeeming power in his children is that he turns greedy, grasping, fearful hoarders into generous, honest, trustworthy givers.

What can you do to live out the positive side of this command before a watching and needy world? If you commit to living not only a life free from stealing, but also to a life characterized by giving, what would your life look like?

A life characterized by giving is a life of diligence. In Ephesians 4:28 Paul says, "Let the thief no longer steal, but rather let him labor, doing honest work with his own hands, so that he may have something to share with anyone in need." Jesus takes thieves and sets them to work. He puts them to work with their hands so that they not only make their own way in life, but they also have something to share with others. He teaches us to "look not only to [our] own interests, but also to the interests of others" (Philippians 2:4).

What is your attitude toward hard work? "In all toil there is profit, but mere talk tends only to poverty" (Proverbs 14:23).

Are you diligent to serve Christ well wherever he has placed you, or are you frequently looking for ways to pamper yourself? "Whatever you do, work heartily, as for the Lord and not for men, knowing that from the Lord you will receive the inheritance as your reward. You are serving the Lord Christ" (Colossians 3:23–24).

Live a life of diligence. Ray's parents have modeled a life of fierce, untiring service to Christ and others. Their passionate love for Christ and their earnest hope of eternal joys with him have fueled their lives with diligence. Mom writes:

> God puts a high level of value on work—all work, and especially eternal work: "Therefore, my beloved brethren, be steadfast, immovable, always abounding in the work of the Lord, knowing that your toil is not in vain in the Lord" (1 Corinthians 15:58). Payday is coming! What is the labor of this little life by comparison? . . . To spend your precious years connecting people with God, influencing them toward heaven by every means we can think of—for this, my friend, don't mind getting totally, gloriously exhausted. We have only a few short years to earn our rewards, and all eternity to enjoy them.[4]

A life characterized by giving is also a life of generosity. The opposite of stealing is generosity. A grateful heart that has been loved by God through the self-accepted poverty of his only Son is, in turn, generous to others, for God "is kind to the ungrateful and the evil" (Luke 6:35). We are told, "Give to everyone who begs from you, and from one who takes away your goods do not demand them back. . . . Give, and it will be given to you. Good measure, pressed down, shaken together, running over, will be put into your lap. For with the measure you use it will be measured back to you" (Luke 6:30, 38). We are also instructed:

> As for the rich in this present age, charge them . . . to do good, to be rich in good works, to be generous and ready to share, thus storing up treasure for themselves as a good foundation for

> the future, so that they may take hold of that which is truly life. (1 Timothy 6:17–19)
>
> You shall not harden your heart or shut your hand against your poor brother, but you shall open your hand to him and lend him sufficient for his need, whatever it may be. . . . You shall give to him freely, and your heart shall not be grudging when you give to him, because for this the LORD your God will bless you in all your work and in all that you undertake. For there will never cease to be poor in the land. Therefore I command you, "You shall open wide your hand to your brother, to the needy and to the poor, in your land." (Deuteronomy 15:7–11)

Christians are called to live a life of generosity. We are to be generous because God has been generous to us. What do we have that we have not received? All of it is from God—a steady job, the health to pursue it, and a heart to receive it from the Lord's own hand.

We are to be generous because we have experienced the redemptive generosity of God. We are to be like the God we serve and to represent him well to others. If all we have is from him and for his use, then we can hold it loosely and share it as he directs because he is the owner; we are the stewards. To live generously means we must have something to share. If we are always working and spending to our limit, what will we have left to give?

Gleaning was an Old Testament principle given to God's children to encourage generosity and prevent theft. God told his people not to harvest their fields right up to the edge nor strip their vineyards of all the fruit. They were to leave these "gleanings" for the poor and for the sojourner (Leviticus 19:10). We have lost this standard for generosity in our push to live life to the very edges. Are we always working, spending, eating, exercising, and vacationing to the limit? We can't be generous if we leave nothing unspent.

At a time when I was pushing at every limit line in my life, my very dear friend and partner in ministry, Melinda, gave me a copy of Richard Swenson's book, *Margin: Restoring Emotional, Physical, Financial, and Time Reserves to Overloaded Lives*. Dr. Swenson defines *margin* as the space that once existed between our limits and our lives in our time, budgets, and emotional and physical energy. That space has been devoured in our push for more. He warns us, "God is honored by funnels, dishonored by sponges. Be a conduit of his blessing, not a dead end."[5]

To be generous is to be redemptive—to give someone what they neither deserve nor can earn, just as we have received from our generous heavenly Father. "For you know the grace of our Lord Jesus Christ, that though he was rich, yet for your sake he became poor, so that you by his poverty might become rich" (2 Corinthians 8:9).

One of the scenes in all of literature that moves me most is from *Les Miserables,* where Jean Valjean is caught stealing the kind bishop's silverware. When the police drag the thief back into the bishop's home, Monseigneur Bienvenu covers for this ex-convict, calling him friend and sending him on his way with the silverware. Much to everyone's shock, the bishop even adds his silver candlesticks (the last of his household valuables), charging Jean Valjean to use these gifts to become an honest man.[6] The rest of the story revolves around the redemptive power of one man's generosity to another. The point is this:

> Whoever sows sparingly will also reap sparingly, and whoever sows bountifully will also reap bountifully. Each one must give as he has decided in his heart, not reluctantly or under compulsion, for God loves a cheerful giver. And God is able to make all grace abound to you, so that having all sufficiency in all things at all times, you may abound in every good work. . . . You will be enriched in every way to be generous in every way, which through us will produce thanksgiving to God. (2 Corinthians 9:6–11)

Giving the Eighth Commandment

Ask any mother of preschoolers and she will tell you that children possess a keen sense of ownership. One of the first words each of our children learned was "mine!" How we need to give this commandment to our children! It is our privilege to teach them the love of their heavenly Father through this commandment. Both with our words and our actions, we must model lives of diligence and generosity.

What is your family's work ethic? Do you require your children to help bear the responsibilities of maintaining your home? Even little children can help with simple chores. Just make sure to use the "Me-Us-You" principle. First it's "Watch me do this." Then it's "Let's do this together." Finally it's "Now you do it." Most of us neglect the "us" part of this principle, which really should bear the biggest emphasis in any teaching. And when we do get to the "now you are ready to take this on by yourself" part, we forget to reward and cheer them on. So our children never learn that hard work brings pleasure and reward.

As we teach our children diligence and generosity, we should talk much of heaven. They must see that while we aren't working *for* heaven, we are striving *toward* heaven. Our labor in the Lord is never in vain (1 Corinthians 15:58). We serve the God who remembers (Hebrews 6:10) as we seek the city that is to come (Hebrews 13:14). And no eye has seen, nor ear heard, nor could we even imagine "what God has prepared for those who love him" (1 Corinthians 2:9). Give your child tiny foretastes of heaven here on earth as you recognize and remember his work, and provide sweet unexpected surprises for a job well done.

Jesus should be your pattern all throughout life. Talk much in your home of Jesus' willingness to become poor for our sakes (2 Corinthians 8:9). Look for ways that your family can become a little poorer so that someone else might become rich for Christ's sake.

Teach your child God's way of generosity from Deuteronomy 24:19–22 and Proverbs 14:21. Who, in the life of your child, is fatherless or a neighbor or sojourner or widow? Plan together how you can experience the joy of not spending and using your resources to the limit so you can share something extra with someone this week. As you live and give "You shall not steal" for those nearest to you, they will come to understand that this commandment is much more than a prohibition. It is an invitation into the very heart of our abundantly generous God.

STUDY AND DISCUSSION FOR LIVING THE EIGHTH COMMANDMENT

1. Take some time to review your memory work. Can you recite the commandments one through eight from memory? How about Psalm 119:18 and Deuteronomy 32:46–47? Memorize this week the final passage for our study of God's loving law. It is found in Matthew 22:37–40. Hide it in your heart. Cherish his Word enough to make it your delight and your counselor (Psalm 119:24).

2. What do you think is at the root of our hearts that tempts us to steal?

3. What kind of God would tell us not to steal but instead to trust him with our every need?

    - Psalm 36:7
    - Hosea 14:4; Revelation 21:6
    - Romans 8:32
    - John 14:1–3
    - 2 Corinthians 8:9
    - 1 Timothy 6:17

4. Read Romans 13:7–10. Are you indebted to anyone for anything either material or spiritual in nature? If so, what does God call you to do about it?

5. Read 1 John 3:16–18. What does your response to the needs of others tell you about the condition of your soul?

6. Each commandment, while telling us what not to do, also implies positive action that we ought to do. How would you state the positive of the eighth commandment? Use these verses to help you think this through.

   - Exodus 23:4–5
   - Ephesians 4:28
   - Matthew 6:38–42
   - 1 Corinthians 6:7–8
   - Acts 18:3–4

7. What is your workload like these days? More than anything it is our attitude about our work that hinders us, even above the work itself. Write out a short biblical work ethic, drawing from these verses:

   - Luke 17:7–10
   - 1 Corinthians 15:58
   - Colossians 3:23–24
   - Hebrews 6:10

8. Read Leviticus 19:9–10; Deuteronomy 24:19–22; Proverbs 14:21. Where in your life is God calling you to leave some margin so you will have something to share? Where do you think God will "bless you in all the work of your hands"?

STUDY AND DISCUSSION FOR GIVING THE EIGHTH COMMANDMENT TO OUR CHILDREN

Materials needed: Bible, marker, and the big red heart.

1. Review with your child the first seven commandments and write the eighth commandment on your big red heart.

2. Talk with your child about possessions. Ask, "If our house caught on fire, but you had time to grab three things as you ran out to safety, what would they be? What really matters in this life?"

3. Make sure your child knows what stealing is. Ask, "Why do people steal? Why is it a sin against God?" Think together about God's providence in your family life. Does your child see everything as coming from God, or does he think you get money by just driving by the bank window whenever you need more (as my four-year-old once told me to do when we were low on funds)?

4. Have you ever been involved in stealing or been violated by someone stealing from you? It may be helpful for your child to hear your story.

5. This commandment is a good springboard for talking about diligence in work. Have you taught your child the beauty of hard work, both by example and requirement? Read Colossians 3:23–24 together. Choose one area you can work on together that needs a more "hearty" approach.

6. Read and discuss with your child 2 Corinthians 8:9. Talk about Jesus' willingness to become poor for our sakes. Is there someone your family knows for whom you could become a little "poorer" so that they might become rich for Jesus' sake? Bring in to your conversation God's love for cheerful giving from 2 Corinthians 9:7.

7. Read together Deuteronomy 24:19–22 and talk about the principle of gleaning. Make a plan to leave a little something extra for someone this week—a shut-in, a neighbor, a teacher, a family member, a secretary, a caregiver, a tradesman. Give your child the opportunity to experience the

joy of not living to every limit of time and energy and money, but having enough to share with those in need of encouragement. Make generosity your word for the week. Be generous yourself. Recognize your child's generosity. You may want to give him the chance to earn some extra money and then pray about who might need it. Let him see that working and sharing and pleasure go hand in hand.

CHAPTER NINE

LOVING THE TRUTH

"You shall not bear false witness against your neighbor."

EXODUS 20:16

HIS LOVING LAW

I confessed in the last chapter that I am a thief. I am also a liar. When I was young (but old enough to know better) my dad had an empty, metal Band-Aid box in his dresser drawer in which he kept his loose change. I discovered it one day while helping my mother put away the clean laundry. Soon I began stealing a nickel here, a dime there. On the way back to school after my lunch break, I'd stop by our neighborhood dime store and stock up on my favorite jawbreakers or Sputnik bubble gum (do you remember those sugary blue gumballs?).

Of course, my friends in the third grade at Robert Fulton Elementary School began to wonder how I had so much money to spend on candy, and soon I was making up various lies to cover my thievery. (The breaking of one commandment seldom stands alone.) Eventually, I grew weary of remembering which lies I had told to whom, and I stopped stealing my dad's change. This episode was not without consequences though. On my next visit to Dr. Patch, our family dentist, I had thirteen cavities to be filled as a result of all that sugar. Ouch!

The Depth of Deceit

What kind of God would tell us that we must not bear false witness against each other? A loving Father, who understands that truth stabilizes relationships. The ninth commandment originally focused against perjuring oneself in a judicial trial. However, Scripture broadens it to include the whole spectrum of lying. God forbids every kind of falsehood (Leviticus 19:11). Honesty, integrity, the reputation of his people—the Lord values these and offers protection and security for his children through this commandment.

But we are liars by nature and live in a culture of lies. Think of all the

- bias in the news;
- misrepresentation among advertisers;
- false promises from politicians;
- slander in the work force;
- gossip over the back fence;
- flattery for our own gain;
- careless laziness to speak the exact truth; and
- even our passive silence when the whole truth is not being told.

We see lying and deceit and self-promotion recorded throughout Scripture, from Genesis 3 to Revelation 22:15. Think back to the garden of Eden. The serpent tempted Eve with deception: "Did God actually say . . . ?" (Genesis 3:1). When Adam and Eve, refusing to heed God's loving law to them, had to answer for their disobedience, they were reduced to finger-pointing and more deception. Adam pointed to Eve, and Eve to the serpent (Genesis 3:11–13). And who of us, when about to be caught in a compromising situation, has not pointed the finger or lied to protect our self-image and reputation?

We all live in the midst of deception and lies. What else can we expect when the Bible teaches that the human race has exchanged the truth about God for a lie, serving the creature rather than the Creator (Romans 1:25)? If we are unwilling to accept the truth about God, then all of life becomes twisted and perverted.

The God of Truth

But God loves us in this command by making truth, purity, and honor the foundation of our life together. God teaches that very thing in Joshua 7 with Achan and again in Acts 5 with Ananias and Sapphira. Both at the beginning of the formation of the nation of Israel and in the early stages of the Christian church, deceivers were punished by God taking away their very lives. Our relationships must be based on trust, authenticity, and faithfulness. And that's where the church comes in. The church of the living God is a "pillar and buttress of the truth" (1 Timothy 3:15). Pillars and buttresses steady and support a building. Truth will be what strengthens and sustains us as the household of God.

What kind of God would decree the ninth commandment? We love and worship the "God of truth" (Isaiah 65:16). Jesus himself said, "I am . . . the truth" (John 14:6). The Holy Spirit is "the Spirit of truth who will guide you into all the truth" (John 16:13). The Bible says that God's words are pure, "like silver . . . purified seven times" (Psalm 12:6). He detests lying lips, but delights in men who are truthful (Proverbs 12:22). God instructs us to speak the truth, rendering judgments that are true and make for peace; we are not to devise evil in our hearts against one another nor love false oaths, for God hates these things (Zechariah 8:16–17).

For all these reasons and more we Christians place ourselves under the judgment of truth because we belong to, and represent to the world, the one who calls himself Truth. This is our God. This is the one who offers himself to us as the delight of our heart. And out of his love for us, he calls us to be truthful.

OUR LASTING LEGACY

Living the Ninth Commandment

But we lie—even as Christians. Paul had to tell the Colossians, "Do not lie to one another, seeing that you have put off the old self with its practices and have put on the new self, which is being renewed in knowledge after the image of its creator" (Colossians 3:9–10).

In order to live out the ninth commandment we need to ask ourselves why we lie. After all, if we know Christ, we are children of the Father of truth. Why would we align ourselves with Satan, "a liar and the father of lies" (John 8:44)?

Why Do We Lie?

Why do we lie? Our immediate answer is that we lie because we are sinners through and through. And that is true. But let's search a little deeper. Sometimes we lie because we are angry and hurt and we want to strike back, so we color the truth a bit, exaggerating to protect ourselves. When I was a child, I once visited a relative whose grown daughter was seeking a divorce. I still remember my shock when this relative told me of her court testimony: "He didn't really throw the alarm clock at her. But I said he did, because that's the only way the judge would grant her a divorce."

Other times we lie because the truth would be too embarrassing to us. "My weight? Oh, around 125 . . ." Sometimes we lie out of fear of the consequences. "I thought the speed limit was 55 mph on this country road, Officer." Another reason we lie is for self-exaltation. We want to make ourselves look better than we really are, such as when we falsify our resume. Other times we just keep silent, which gives the false impression that a circulating lie is the truth. Or we hide the truth. "Do I really need to declare that honorarium as income?" We are spring-loaded to do the work of the devil and then find some way to rationalize it.

How Can We Stop?

Our behavior is always rooted in what we believe. All our behavior stems from our heartfelt belief that either *Jesus is enough* or *Jesus is not enough*, so we must somehow fill the void that he won't or can't. There is more to being a Christian than asking Jesus into our hearts. Belief in his goodness and watch-care and love for us will have its full effect when we feel loved and cared for from our hearts.

For instance, if I say that I believe that God cares about me and is sovereign over my whole life in mercy and love, yet I am held captive by various fears, I don't really believe that God is good. My belief in his sovereign control is only an intellectual concept, not a heartfelt belief. *Head knowledge is never enough to stop sin; only heart-love is.* I sin because something or someone is more significant to me at that moment. When we sin, we are finding our meaning or security in something other than God. He is the one who made us and knows us and loved us so much that he submitted to torture at the hands of liars who brought false testimony against the only perfectly truthful person in the universe.

When we stop trusting God, we start forging our own way, and then we become very dangerous. After all, the devils believe in God (James 2:19). But they don't *love* God, and that's the difference. That is why heartfelt love for God is our deepest need. Our hearts need to be thrilled with the God of truth.

How does this happen? I can't just tell myself to believe. I need to learn how to preach the gospel to myself. I need to expose myself to the beauty and love of God over and over again in study and teaching and meditation and music and fellowship and prayer. Jesus tells us that all things are possible to one who believes. Are you weak here, as I am? Then let's cry out to him, "I believe; help my unbelief!" (Mark 9:23–24).

How does this relate to the ninth commandment? If we love God for being a truthful God—if our heart is delighted with the beauty of the God of truth—we will be less inclined to lie. But if this article of faith holds a place only in our minds and hasn't won our hearts, we will lie easily. Remember, head knowledge doesn't stop sin; only heartfelt love does.

Our Poisonous Tongues

What is God's will for us in the ninth commandment? The Heidelberg Catechism answers our question this way:

> God's will is that I never give false testimony against anyone, twist no one's words, not gossip or slander, nor join in condemning anyone without a hearing or without a just cause. Rather in court and everywhere else, I should avoid lying and deceit of every kind; these are devices the devil himself uses, and they would call down on me God's intense anger. I should love the truth, speak it candidly, and openly acknowledge it. And I should do what I can to guard and advance my neighbor's good name.[1]

Every word we speak should be solid, trustworthy, and real. We must be people who ask ourselves hard questions about what we say and how we represent matters to others. Does what we say bring beauty and grace to those who hear? Our words should be life giving and nourishing. "The tongue of the righteous is choice silver . . . the lips of the righteous feed many" (Proverbs 10:20–21). But so often this is not the case. Our tongues spew forth venom as we casually let our opinions be known. Thomas Watson said, "The scorpion carries poison in his tail, the slanderer carries poison in his tongue."[2]

James 3 describes that although the tongue is such a small part of our body, it reveals how well we control the rest. "If anyone does not stumble in what he says, he is able also to bridle his whole body . . . but no human being can tame the tongue. It is a restless evil, full of deadly poison" (v. 2, 8).

How we need God's help here! "If a report is unnecessary and unkind, and if it might just be a little exaggerated in our own tongue's rendering of how we render it with our tongue, and if it might become more exaggerated in the retelling of it the next time, we'd better be silent about it. It is my tongue and your tongue that is likened to a bucking horse that is running away with its rider. It is my tongue and your tongue that is likened to the ship tossing on the waves with the rudder not properly in the hands of the expert."[3] The Bible tells us to guard our venomous tongues:

> Set a guard, O LORD, over my mouth; keep watch over the door of my lips! (Psalm 141:3)
>
> Whoever guards his mouth preserves his life; he who opens wide his lips comes to ruin. (Proverbs 13:3)
>
> Finally, all of you, have unity of mind, sympathy, brotherly love, a tender heart, and a humble mind. Do not repay evil for evil or reviling for reviling, but on the contrary, bless, for to this you were called, that you may obtain a blessing. For "Whoever desires to love life and see good days, let him keep his tongue from evil and his lips from speaking deceit; let him turn away from evil and do good; let him seek peace and pursue it. For the eyes of the Lord are on the righteous, and his ears are open to their prayer. But the face of the Lord is against those who do evil." (1 Peter 3:8–12)

A Promise of Grace

What is the positive of this command? Each commandment implies a promise of grace. As God fulfills his promise of grace in us, our mouths will be filled with his praises and the truth of God. Our tongues will bring forth justice and honor and wisdom and gladness and healing. We will feel so secure in our own justification through Christ that we'll feel no need to put others down. We will feel so cared for by our heavenly Father that we won't need to lie to save those extra dollars. And we'll feel so humbled by his saving love for us that we won't need to exaggerate to save face. God's gracious heartfelt love will be the guard over our thoughts and words (Ephesians 4:29–32).

When God's purposes are all fulfilled and all wrongs finally righted, God will bear a true witness about his servants. When friends or family slander or even abandon us, we remain in good company—Jeremiah, Paul, and other heroic people. Remember, God will have the last word about us, and he will bear a true witness about our godly hearts and our true worth.

So we can learn to bear up under false accusations. "When reviled, we bless; when persecuted, we endure; when slandered, we entreat" (1 Corinthians 4:12–13). Jesus did. In fact, it was false witnesses whose testimony sentenced him to death (Matthew 26:57–62). Even during his agony on the cross, he did not lash out. The Bible says that Jesus entrusted himself to him who judges rightly (1 Peter 2:23). We can, too.

Giving the Ninth Commandment

How can you pass down a legacy of truth telling to your children? First, don't let gossip buzz around your house. Don't listen to it, and don't share it. Let no one wonder, "Is my name safe in your house?" The Bible says that love covers over an offense (Proverbs 17:9). Often silence is the blanket of love needed to let a tale die down.

Second, make it as easy as possible for others to tell you the truth, especially young children. If possible, avoid direct questions such as "Did you take that money?" or "Why did you hit your brother?" Anyone will lie to protect himself. After all, what is he supposed to say? "I hit him because I am a sinner—totally depraved and unable to control the anger I feel in my little heart!" Of course he will want to defend himself! Comments like, "Tell me about this," or, "Let's go help Jimmy—he's really crying," can open the way for honesty and sincere apologies.

Third, utilize good literature to teach honesty to your children. Among books that I have found helpful are *Sam, Bangs, and Moonshine* by Evaline Ness, *The Children's Book of Virtues* and *The Children's Book of Heroes*, edited by William Bennett, and *George Washington* and *Abraham Lincoln* by Ingri and Edgar Parin D'Aulaire.

Finally, and most importantly, we must be truth tellers ourselves. When we lie, we must be humble enough to confess it and make it right. We must do all we can to let honesty, kindness, and love govern our spheres of influence. Only then will we leave a lasting legacy of truth.

STUDY AND DISCUSSION FOR LIVING THE NINTH COMMANDMENT

1. Recite from memory the first nine commandments. Write out your memory verses:

    - Psalm 119:18
    - Deuteronomy 32:46–47
    - Matthew 22:37–40

2. What do these verses tell us about God and why he would give us the ninth commandment?

    - John 14:6
    - John 18:37
    - Psalm 12:6
    - Proverbs 6:16–19
    - Zechariah 8:16–17

3. Read Joshua 7:1–26 and Acts 5:1–11. Why would God judge these people so severely?

4. What does it mean that the church is "the pillar and buttress of truth" (1 Timothy 3:15)?

5. Why do you think people lie? Why do you lie?

6. What is the positive side of the ninth commandment? See Proverbs 10:20–21 and 1 Peter 3:8–12.

7. What should our response be when someone lies to us or about us? See 1 Corinthians 4:12–13 and 1 Peter 2:23.

8. Use these verses for prayer and meditation:

    - Psalm 119:29
    - Psalm 141:3
    - Proverbs 11:13
    - Proverbs 19:1
    - 1 Corinthians 13:4–7
    - Ephesians 4:29–32

STUDY AND DISCUSSION FOR GIVING THE NINTH COMMANDMENT TO OUR CHILDREN

Materials needed: marker, Bible, picture of someone known for honesty (you could even use a coin or bill with a picture of George Washington or Abraham Lincoln), tape, and the big red heart.

1. Review the first eight commandments with your child, then add the ninth commandment and write it on your big red heart.

2. Read an age-appropriate story about truth telling to your child. (See books listed at the end of this chapter for suggestions.) Talk about the beauty and security of honesty. If you can find a picture of someone known for honesty, tape it near this command.

3. Do you have a personal experience you could share with your child about a time when it was hard for you to tell the truth? Did you lie? Why? How did you feel? Were there any consequences? Talk about why people (even children) lie.

4. Discuss what kind of God we serve and how that should affect our speech. Read together John 14:6; 18:37 and Proverbs 6:16–19.

5. Read with your child Psalm 101:7; Proverbs 19:5; and Matthew 12:36–37. Discuss what kind of warnings God gives us about lying. Help your child to see that a pattern of lying drives her away from the presence of the God of truth.

6. As a parent or teacher it is your responsibility to open the way for a child to tell the truth. What child would not tell a lie to escape certain punishment (George Washington was an exception!)? Think of how you should interact when you suspect your child might be tempted to lie. Word your questions very carefully so as to give her a way to redeem the situation without having to lie.

7. Model truth to your child. Do all that you can to see that honesty, kindness, and love govern the speech in your spheres of influence.

REAL CONTENTMENT

"You shall not covet."

EXODUS 20:17

HIS LOVING LAW

The tenth commandment speaks directly to our hearts. The other nine commandments tell us what to do and what not to do, and could be reduced to mere behavioral norms, all too often in a self-righteous way. But this commandment, rather than forbidding an action, forbids a state of mind—an attitude of the heart. This commandment makes me ask myself the question, "What do I really want in life?"

Covetousness Is Misplaced Desire

Remember that the first commandment says, "You shall have no other gods before me." In other words, "You shall have, love, treasure, prize, and relish ME!" The tenth commandment says, "You shall not covet," or, in other words, "Let me fill your heart so full that you desire nothing else for your ultimate happiness." Both commandments speak about idols. Do you remember our definition of an idol? An idol is anything we need besides God to make us happy.

Colossians 3:5 says, "Put to death therefore what is earthly in you: sexual immorality, impurity, passion, evil desire, and covetousness, *which is idolatry.*" God hates idols because when they are present in our lives, we are really saying, "God, you just aren't enough for me. I need something more from you. For me to be happy you must be more generous or more kind or more rewarding or more understanding or more . . ."

This offends God. Covetousness is a spiritual problem. Our lives aren't full enough or fun enough or good enough. God isn't answering our prayers in the way we want him to for that husband, or for that expanded budget, or for that much-needed vacation. We live in a consumer culture, and consumption has become a way of life. Whenever we think, "I wish I had her ____," we are dealing with this heart sin of breaking the tenth commandment.

And this doesn't just apply to material possessions—clothes, houses, furniture, cars, and vacations. It can also apply to intelligence, family connections, and energy levels. It can apply to invitations to events, to control over the lives of our grown children, to musical talent, career recognition, influence, power, beauty—you name it. The list is endless.

The tenth commandment does not forbid the desire to improve our lot in life; it forbids envying my neighbor's ability to improve his lot in life. It condemns the comparison game. "Why did she get that? Aren't I just as deserving?"

One of Aesop's fables tells us of the covetous man to whom Zeus would grant any wish on condition that his neighbor would get twice as much of it. Unable to bear the thought of his neighbor's good fortune, the man wished to lose one eye![1] Desire itself is not our problem. God made us for desire. He made us to long after, to yearn for, and to stretch out for great, eternal things. In Psalm 19:10 the psalmist tells us the judgments of the Lord are more to be *desired* than gold, even much fine gold.

Desire itself is not our problem. Our problem is *misplaced desire*. This commandment does not forbid our desiring a husband or home or child or job. But we are not to lust after our neighbor's husband or home or child or job. This commandment takes us right down to the deepest interior of our beings to see where our desires are really focused.

How God Loves Us in This Commandment

God loves us in this commandment by helping us see that as long as we are seeking our happiness in things and people and circumstances, we will never find real satisfaction. Things break, people disappoint, and circumstances inevitably change. And so he warns us not to hunger after these things.

God knows what we really want, not just what we think we want. He sees into our very hearts and tells us not to covet so that we learn to deal with our restless discontent. God knows our hearts. He knows they tell the truth of who we really are. The tenth commandment is a mirror to our souls, revealing—if we look carefully enough—our view of God amidst all our misplaced desire.

What Is It about God I Don't Understand?

When I am tempted toward covetousness, I need to ask myself, "What is it about God that I don't understand in this situation? Why isn't God enough for me here?" For many years the focus of my heart was a car. We lived in Scotland for four years while Ray earned his PhD at the University of Aberdeen. We had sold our house and furniture and appliances and car, and we had invested everything with a reputable Christian investor to finance the study project. The month our fourth child was born, our investor went belly-up and we had to sell our car. For two years, as I walked back and forth to our village for food and medicine, took buses into Aberdeen for clothes and Christmas gifts, and walked to and from church every Sunday with four young children, I coveted a car. I made a deal with God. If he would give us a car, I would be happy!

Well, two years later, he did, through our generous parents. But was I happy? Sure, I was, for a few months. But we had a hard time fitting all six of us into it. Their gift really wasn't big enough for our growing family. So now I was coveting a minivan. Eventually we were able to get a minivan, and we all fit so nicely into it. But by then I was a suburban soccer mom with a full-time job teaching school and four kids to carpool around, plus I had responsibilities with Ray's job and various ministry opportunities. Was I happy with our minivan? No; now I was coveting a *second* car. "Any car would do, Lord, and I promise you—this time, I will truly be happy!"

Was it wrong for me to want a car? Was it wrong for me to desire a second car? Not necessarily, but this desire had begun to overrule my heart. God was not enough for me. The problem was my misplaced desire. I wasted so much spiritual energy desiring a car! The root of my covetousness was my distrust of God's providence for our family.

What does your life consist of? When you peel away the layers of niceness, and social charms, and the care to make a good impression, what occupies your heart and mind and soul? What do you daydream about, plan for, rejoice over? "Take care, and be on your guard against all covetousness, for one's life does not consist in the abundance of his possessions" (Luke 12:15).

OUR LASTING LEGACY

Living the Tenth Commandment

Let's nurture a vital, satisfying relationship with Jesus Christ. Let's not be women who stifle our desires. Let's be women who *feed our godly desires*. Our spiritual lives are won or lost at the level of our hearts. "Faith not only purifies the heart, but satisfies it; it makes God our portion and in him we have enough."[2] What do we really want in life and in death? Is Jesus Christ, in all his love and grace, enough for us?

Remember that God knows our hearts. He knows they tell the truth about who we really are (1 John 3:19–20). That's why he gave us the tenth commandment. He wants us to look deep inside our very hearts and see that even there we need a Redeemer. Even if we could keep all the other commandments, this one is impossible! Who has ever lived a life never once thinking, "If I had ____, my life would be so much better. Then I could really be happy"?

But God knows how to do the impossible. He can change the human heart so that we trust him with all our lives—every detail—right down to what occupies the "desire setting" in our souls. He is in the business of transforming self-centered, self-serving, self-loving human beings into Christ-honoring, Christ-serving, Christ-loving people. God, through the power of the Holy Spirit, can fill our hearts with so much love for him that there is no room left for jealousy and covetousness.

> And God is able to make all grace abound to you, so that having all sufficiency in all things at all times, you may abound in every good work. (2 Corinthians 9:8)

> The LORD is my shepherd; I shall not want. (Psalm 23:1)

> I have learned in whatever situation I am to be content. (Philippians 4:11)

The positive side of this commandment is contentment. It's learning to live with a sense of God's impending goodness. You never know what goodness God is going to pour out on you. Maybe he will provide that car you need, or maybe he will give you the grace you need to live faithfully without one. Maybe he will heal your loved one, or maybe he will comfort you in your loss in ways you never thought possible this side of heaven. Maybe he will answer your prayer just as you thought he should, but maybe he will grace you in ways so rewarding that, looking back on them, you will even praise him for that unanswered prayer.

Psalm 31:19 says, "Oh, how abundant is your goodness, which you have stored up for those who fear you and worked for those who take refuge in you." When you live in that expectation and awareness, covetousness fades. Instead of asking yourself, "Why did God ____?" you begin anticipating what good thing God has stored up for you in this situation. What is he working as you take your refuge in him?

This is a radical approach to life. You will only find it in the Bible. In fact, even the apostle Paul had to learn it. In Philippians 4:11–12 he says, "I have learned in whatever situation I am to be content. . . . I have learned the secret of facing plenty and hunger, abundance and need." Contentment is a *learned* behavior.

What does contentment mean? It certainly does *not* mean folding your hands and acquiescing to difficult situations that truly need to be improved. But there is a sense in which, by God's grace, you can be content *in* a situation while not being content *with* it. For instance, you can learn to be content *in* your job, while not being content *with* it. Contentment does not mean that you will never change jobs. But it does mean that you will cast your cares on God, choosing to trust his goodness, and letting his peace rule in your heart as you pray and seek his will.

You can learn to be content *in* your home, while not being content *with* it. It is not wrong to redecorate or improve your home. But it does mean you will not let this become the focus of your heart until your house is picture perfect.

You can learn to be content *in* your marriage while not being content *with* it. I always want to go deeper with Ray, loving and supporting him more today than I did yesterday.

I can learn to be content *in* my physical limitations right now with one ruptured and two bulging discs while not being content *with* them as I strive to exercise properly and do everything I can to help the healing process.

Contentment is a learned grace. You can't just decide one day that you won't covet anymore. Your heart was made to covet, because God made your heart an organ of deep desire, and it demands to be filled with something. Your heart cannot remain empty, blank, and desireless. The cure for covetousness is to learn to covet the right things.

Notice that this commandment does not simply say, "Don't covet." It says, "Don't covet your neighbor's possessions and prizes." There are certain things we *can* covet, however; *there is a godly coveting*. We just need to learn to covet the right things—an insatiable appetite for Christ: his grace, his mercy, his nearness. We can fill our hearts with the goodness of God. "He who did not spare his own Son but gave him up for us all, how will he not also with him graciously give us all things?" (Romans 8:32). "No good thing does he withhold from those who walk uprightly" (Psalm 84:11). "My God will supply every need of yours according to his riches in glory in Christ Jesus" (Philippians 4:19).

God is telling us that whatever we have, we need, and whatever we don't have, we don't need. We don't need more things, better health, or a new job as much as we need more of God! The tenth commandment entices us back to where we started in the first commandment, with God himself as our first priority and deepest delight. God wants our hearts to be filled with himself. "Delight yourself in the LORD, and he will give you the desires of your heart" (Psalm 37:4).

Giving the Tenth Commandment

Contentment is such a rare quality today, especially in our children. How can we help them foster hearts that covet the things of eternity rather than the passing fads of this world? First of all, we can ask God to help us set an example. Have our children ever seen us go happily without something we really wanted? We can help our child see in us a godly coveting, a coveting for spiritual treasures that far surpass anything here on earth. As we nurture a vital, fulfilling relationship with Jesus Christ, we will covet him more and more, and godly contentment will be the fruit of our lives. Our children will hear us say, and see us live out, "If I have Jesus, I have all that I need."

Let your children see you happy for the good fortune of others. Are you raising them in an atmosphere that exudes the contentment of real humility and deep joy in someone else's success? Can you truly say with Christ, "It is more blessed to give than to receive"? (Acts 20:35). Teach them stories of contentment from the Bible. The letters of Paul are a good place to start. Read 2 Corinthians 11:23–33 and then turn to Philippians 4:11–13. Let your child see that contentment is learned through drawing close to Christ. Is Christ the joy of your heart? Can you say with David, "There is nothing on earth that I desire besides you" (Psalm 73:25)? What you love reveals whom you love (1 John 2:15–17).

For your child to understand this commandment, she will have to begin to delight in Christ on her own, not just because you want her to. Pray for the soul of your child. Ask God to turn your child's heart to him in real love and wonder. Don't try to squelch her cravings—her heart was created to yearn. But in wisdom and patience let her experience the hollowness of the world's offerings.

Ask God to help your child at the root level of his sin, the motivational level. Is he learning to hate his sin because he got caught or because it offends his heavenly Father? Only God can pierce his heart with saving love. You might be able to change his outward behavior—at least while he lives in your home. But only God can change his heart to want to follow Christ once he is on his own.

When we lived in Augusta, Georgia, our side yard was rampant with briers. One summer I was so frustrated with them, I took to cutting them back. How silly of me. I wanted a quick fix. You know what happened—my impatience only made them grow more. I needed to get to their roots if I ever was to stop their speedy growth. So it is with sin. You may be able to help control your child's outward behavior, but only God can change his heart.

Pray, model, pray some more, teach him the Bible, pray again, discipline him, pray, surround him with other believers at a good church, pray, and then keep on praying. God answers prayer.

STUDY AND DISCUSSION FOR LIVING THE TENTH COMMANDMENT

1. Can you recite from memory all ten commandments? Try to write them out. Say your three memory verse passages to a friend or family member.

2. What *if onlys* have you struggled with? Explain these statements: "The heart manufactures idols," and "Our spiritual lives are won or lost at the level of our hearts."

3. Contented souls do not covet. The cure for covetousness is the positive of this command. Can you state it? Read Romans 8:32, Philippians 4:11–13, and Hebrews 13:5.

4. Read James 4:1–6 and Psalm 16:5–11. How can you help foster contentment in your home and spheres of influence?

STUDY AND DISCUSSION FOR GIVING THE TENTH COMMANDMENT TO OUR CHILDREN

Materials needed: Bible, marker, 2 small plants or weeds with the roots still intact, baggie (or you could use sweet potatoes, 6 toothpicks, and 2 small glass jars), and the big red heart.

1. Write the tenth commandment on your big red heart. Recite with your child all ten commandments.

2. Read 1 John 2:15–17. Discuss what it means to "love the world." *What* you and your child love reveals *whom* you love. Are toys, food, money, popularity, power, or beauty more appealing and rewarding than loving and following Jesus Christ? Take time to pray this through with your child, being open and honest about some of your own struggles.

3. To understand this commandment, your child needs to be lifted above his heart's desires and given new, bigger desires. Does your child know about heaven? Read together John 14:1–3 and Revelation 21:1–4. Talk about people your child knew who have gone before him into heaven. Tell him your own anticipation of going there someday.

4. This commandment pertains to the heart. Try to find two plants with big root systems. Weeds are a good choice to use in the summer time; a sweet potatoes suspended in water would work well in the winter. If it is summer, go out and pull up two weeds, leaving the root intact on one weed and simply cutting off the top of the plant on the other, leaving the root to reproduce. Talk about whether these weeds will die. Put one in a baggie and save it near your big red heart. Come back in a few weeks to see what has happened to the weed with roots left in the ground. Ask your child, "Why do you think this weed grew, while the other weed died?"

   If you are doing this during the winter, talk about the different parts of a plant, teaching your child that the potato is the root of the plant. Pierce each potato with enough toothpicks to hold it above a glass jar filled with water, allowing a small portion of the potato to be submerged. Put it near a window that lets direct sunlight through, and wait for several days. After some leaves have grown, take one out of the water, cut off its leaves, and wait to see if they grow back. Compare the two potatoes. Help your child to understand that the root is where the plant gets its food to sustain its life. As long as the root survives, the plant can grow. If the root is not fed, the plant cannot grow. Help your child compare the human heart to the root. What is he feeding his heart? What can he expect to grow there?

5. Read together Philippians 4:11–13 and 2 Corinthians 11:23–33. Talk about contentment. Point out the verb *learned* from the Philippians passage. Discuss how one learns contentment. Tell your child how God has helped you learn to be content. Pray together, asking God to fill your hearts with himself. Give your child completely to God, asking him to use your child in whatever ways would best serve the purposes of God.

CONCLUSION

JESUS, PRICELESS TREASURE

There is a walk I love to take in Percy Warner Park here in Nashville, Tennessee. It winds for almost six miles through beautiful wooded hills filled with deer and owls and other forest creatures. Along the path there is a huge, hollowed-out, old tree trunk still standing from decades past. In the spring one can find a few leaves trying to grow from it, but mostly it is barren, a home for various critters and a hideout for children to play in.

I often think of the Ten Commandments when I see this tree trunk. It paints for me a picture of the Ten Commandments in the lives of so many: the trunk of our beliefs remains standing, but there is little growth or vibrancy in our root system. I wonder how we will withstand the first big storm that comes along. What legacy are we leaving for our children?

When we look at the Ten Commandments, we often see them as a list of rules, a strict code of righteousness passed down for thousands of years from an ancient and rather demanding God. We feel an exacting and unrelenting pressure to be and feel things that we can't seem to drum up. Have you ever been there? If so, congratulations, because that feeling is what the law is all about!

The law is meant to show us our deep internal need. It is only able to condemn. It can never save. Why? The law cannot save because holiness never comes from behavior modification. It only flows out from fullness of the Holy Spirit. Spiritual life is never validated by external behavior alone, but by the radiant inner delight of a heart made new in Christ.

We saw at the beginning of our study that God, through his love and sacrifice, has brought us out of our personal land of slavery to serve him. Each human heart will serve something, because our hearts are created to serve. We will either serve our Creator or the one he created. Each commandment brings us to a fork in the road—not a barrier, but an open door. What will life be like in the next generation as we live the Ten Commandments and give them to our children? Will it be like Pottersville or Bedford Falls?

What is God's purpose in the law? What does it mean to us today? What change does it undergo in the New Testament? Let's review some of what we have learned, remembering that "the law is good, if one uses it lawfully" (1 Timothy 1:8).

Under the old covenant, the people of Israel were in an *if . . . then* relationship with God. *If* they obeyed him, *then* there would be blessing. But they failed. They couldn't do it on their own. In the new covenant, God promises to write his law on our hearts (Jeremiah 31:33). The new covenant doesn't do away with the law; it internalizes it (Romans 8:3–4). God has done what the law never could do.

In the old covenant, God *tells* me to be good; for example, "You shall not steal." In the new covenant, he *enables* me to be good. He knows I can't, so he gives me a generous heart through Christ.

Under the old covenant, I believe God will love me more if I am good. The old covenant says, "I obey, therefore I am accepted." But the new covenant says, "I am accepted, therefore I obey." God cannot possibly love me any more than he already does through Christ. I am totally depraved and just as totally loved (Romans 5:8).

The old covenant says friendship with God means perfection.

The new covenant tells us that friendship with God means brokenness. The old covenant law keeper says, "I did it!" The new covenant law keeper says, "Christ did it!" In passing on this wonderful legacy of God's loving law, parents should deploy the old covenant—"You must honor me by making your bed"—while teaching the new covenant—"I know you're running late this morning. Let me come help you make it."

You may be thinking, is the law obsolete? Is it even unchristian? No, no, never no! Let me quote a Puritan father to help us here. Samuel Bolton tells us of the working relationship between the law and the cross, the circle of the old and new covenants. He says:

> The law sends us to the gospel that we may be justified. And the gospel sends us to the law again to inquire what is our duty as those who are justified. The law sends us to the gospel for our justification; the gospel sends us to the law to frame our way of life.[1]

Do you remember our analogy of the law as a mirror? The mirror of the law shows us our sin but can never cleanse us. The cross of Jesus Christ is the only place in the whole universe to find cleansing.

The Ten Commandments tell us what God would look like if he were human. And sixteen hundred years after giving them to his people, God did come to earth as a man to live a life of perfect obedience. More than anyone, Jesus is the one who teaches us to obey the will of God. When we look at him, in light of our own efforts, our deeply rooted self-justification is silenced. Our hearts' desire to look and, indeed, be superior is quelled in humility and gratitude.

Jesus says, "If you love me, you will keep my commandments" (John 14:15). If we kept his commandments perfectly, what would we look like?

1) We would always be satisfied with God—he would be enough.

2) We would always worship God perfectly with no idols to crowd our hearts.

3) We would hallow God's name perfectly because of our deep delight in him, living like we really are Christians.

4) We would have a God-centered schedule.

5) We would overflow with gratitude and respect for our parents.

6) We would be life givers, always breathing life into others.

7) We would joyfully honor every marriage vow and build marriages full of holy romance.

8) We would be generous, always looking for ways to give to others.

9) We would defend others, always eager that the truth be well represented.

10) We would always be satisfied with God, deeply content in our inner being.

Jesus says, "If you love me, you will keep my commandments." Do you love Jesus? Well, do you delight to do his commandments? Do you see them as a "get to" not a "have to"? Are you becoming more and more like him? You become like the one you admire (2 Kings 17:14–15).

Let's be women who come to him, asking him to fill us with so much of himself that we begin to delight in following our individual pathways to heaven. Let the law have its natural impact. Let's not be afraid to see our own smallness compared to what we should be. Moral failure is not the worst that can happen to us. Moral success can keep us from Christ.

Let's stop prizing our moral superiority and let's learn to prize Christ. He is the one who fulfills the law perfectly. He will write his law on our hearts, and in him we will be able to obey God. God's invitation reads: "Let Jesus be your moral legitimacy. He earned it by keeping my law perfectly and paying the price of all your failures. Through my grace I give you his perfect standing."

When Satan tempts me to despair
And tells me of the guilt within
Upward I look and see him there
Who made an end of all my sin.
Because the sinless Savior died

My sinful soul is counted free
For God, the Just, was satisfied
To look on him and pardon me,
To look on him and pardon me.[2]

His loving law—have you come to feel his love in these commandments? Our lasting legacy—will you join me and others in living it out, through the grace and merit of Jesus Christ, before a watching world? Our children need you. So does the world. God bless you.

CONCLUSION

STUDY AND DISCUSSION FOR LIVING THE TEN COMMANDMENTS AND GIVING THEM TO OUR CHILDREN

These final questions can be done together with your child. You will need the big red heart for review.

1. Review the Ten Commandments and your memory verses. Remember that these are not just a set of rules. The Ten Commandments reflect who God is and what kind of people he wants us to become.

2. Talk about different responses people can have to God's law:

   - We can be angry at ourselves: "I can never get this right."
   - We can be angry at God: "He demands too much for me to follow him."
   - We can be angry at our sin: "I'll turn to Jesus for his help and forgiveness."

   Which one is the biblical response?

3. Think about how God loves us through each law. Try to write the positive of each commandment.

   - The first commandment:
   - The second commandment:
   - The third commandment:
   - The fourth commandment:
   - The fifth commandment:
   - The sixth commandment:
   - The seventh commandment:
   - The eighth commandment:
   - The ninth commandment:
   - The tenth commandment:

Remember that friendship with God is not perfection; it is striving to please him, but when we don't please him, we turn to him for forgiveness and help. As we do, we'll become more and more like him until one day in heaven we'll be with him and never struggle with sin again.

4. Spend some time in prayer, thanking God for his loving law and for his Son, who kept it perfectly for you. Ask him to keep writing it on your heart until you see him face-to-face, when you will be totally free to love and honor him perfectly.

NOTES

Introduction

1. Donald Grey Barnhouse, *Exposition of Bible Doctrines: Taking the Epistle to the Romans as a Point of Departure* (Grand Rapids, MI: Eerdmans, 1953), 275–76.
2. Susan Hunt, an influential author in my denomination (Presbyterian Church in America [PCA]), has helped me understand that children are a product of their theology.
3. Philip Graham Ryken, *Written in Stone: The Ten Commandments and Today's Moral Crisis* (Wheaton, IL: Crossway, 2003), 29.
4. Jochem Douma, *The Ten Commandments: Manual for the Christian Life* (Phillipsburg, NJ: P&R, 1996), 7.

Chapter 1

1. William Kilpatrick, "Faith & Therapy," *First Things,* February 1999, 23.
2. See Ezekiel 16 and Ephesians 5:22–33. For an in-depth study of this theme throughout the whole span of Scripture, see Raymond C. Ortlund Jr., *God's Unfaithful Wife: A Biblical Theology of Spiritual Adultery* (Downer's Grove, IL: InterVarsity Press, 2002).
3. Os Guinness and John Seel, *No God but God: Breaking with the Idols of our Age* (Chicago: Moody Press, 1992), 32–33.
4. Matthew Henry, *Commentary on the Whole Bible: Genesis to Deuteronomy* (McClean, VA: McDonald, n.d.), 1:358.
5. Quoted in Michael S. Horton, *The Law of Perfect Freedom* (Chicago: Moody Press, 1993), 56.
6. Raymond C. Ortlund Sr., *Lord, Make My Life a Miracle!* (Ventura, CA: Regal Books, 1974).
7. Westminster Confession of Faith, The Larger Catechism (Glasgow: Bell and Bain, 1995), 186–87.

Chapter 2

1. Matthew Henry, *Commentary on the Whole Bible: Genesis to Deuteronomy* (McClean, VA: McDonald, n.d.), 1:359.

2. J. I. Packer, *Knowing God* (Downers Grove, IL: InterVarsity Press, 1973), 42.
3. V. Gerald Janzen, *Exodus* (Louisville, KY: Westminster John Knox Press, 1997), 147.
4. I thank my dear husband, Ray, for his insights here.

Chapter 3

1. J. D. Douglas, ed., *The New Bible Dictionary* (Grand Rapids, MI: Eerdmans, 1973), 862–63.
2. Jochem Douma, *The Ten Commandments: Manual for the Christian Life* (Phillipsburg, NJ: P&R, 1996), 83.

Chapter 4

1. See Herbert Danby, "Shabbath," in *The Mishnah* (Oxford: Oxford University Press, rprt. 1977), 100ff; Alfred Edersheim, *The Life and Times of Jesus the Messiah* (Grand Rapids, MI: Eerdmans, rprt. 1973), 2:777–87.
2. Thomas Watson, *The Ten Commandments* (Edinburgh: Banner of Truth, rprt. 1982), 99.

Chapter 5

1. Philip Graham Ryken, *Written in Stone: The Ten Commandments and Today's Moral Crisis* (Wheaton, IL: Crossway, 2003), 131.

Chapter 6

1. Pat Robertson, *The Ten Offenses* (Nashville, TN: Integrity, 2004), 36.

2 David Grossman, "Trained to Kill," *Christianity Today,* August 19, 1998, 2–3.

3. Edith Schaeffer, *Lifelines: The Ten Commandments for Today* (Wheaton, IL: Crossway, 1982), 122.
4. Thomas Watson, *The Ten Commandments* (Edinburgh: Banner of Truth, rprt. 1981), 138.

Chapter 7

1. Sara Teasdale, "Appraisal," in Elisabeth Elliot, *Let Me Be a Woman* (Wheaton, IL: Tyndale, 1976), 81.

CHAPTER 8

1. Philip Graham Ryken, *Written in Stone: The Ten Commandments and Today's Moral Crisis* (Wheaton, IL: Crossway, 2003), 171.
2. "Othello," 3.3, *The Complete Works of Shakespeare* (New York: Crown Publishers, 1979), 3:678.
3. Many of these ideas came from R. Kent Hughes, *Disciplines of Grace* (Wheaton, IL: Crossway, 1993), 144ff.
4. Anne Ortlund, *Disciplines of the Beautiful Woman* (Waco, TX: Word, 1977), 37–38.
5. Richard A. Swenson, *Margin: Restoring Emotional, Physical, Financial, and Time Reserves to Overloaded Lives* (Colorado Springs, CO: NavPress, 1992), 179.
6. Victor Hugo, *Les Miserables* (New York: Penguin, 1987), 103–5.

CHAPTER 9

1. Heidelberg Catechism, Question 112, Ecumenical Creed and Reformed Confession (Grand Rapids, MI: Board of Publications of the Christian Reformed Church, 1979), 54.
2. Thomas Watson, *The Ten Commandments* (Edinburgh: Banner of Truth, rprt. 1981), 169.
3. Edith Schaeffer, *Lifelines* (Wheaton, IL: Crossway, 1982), 189.

CHAPTER 10

1. See Joy Davidman, *Smoke on the Mountain* (Philadelphia: Westminster, 1953), 120.
2. Thomas Watson, *The Ten Commandments* (Edinburgh: Banner of Truth, rprt. 1981), 179.

CONCLUSION

1. Samuel Bolton, in Philip Graham Ryken, *Written in Stone: The Ten Commandments and Today's Moral Crisis* (Wheaton, IL: Crossway, 2003), 225.
2. Charlie Lee Bancroft and Vikki Cook, "Before the Throne of God Above" (PDI Worship, 1993).

Personal Reflections